Effective
Communications

Effective
Communications

Get your message across and learn how to listen

STEVE SHIPSIDE

**LONDON, NEW YORK,
MUNICH, MELBOURNE, and DELHI**

Produced for Dorling Kindersley
by **terry jeavons&company**

Project Editor	Fiona Biggs
Project Art Editor	Terry Jeavons
Designer	J. C. Lanaway
Special Photography	Mike Hemsley
Senior Editor	Simon Tuite
Editor	Tom Broder
US Editor	Margaret Parrish
Senior Art Editor	Sara Robin
DTP Designer	Traci Salter
Production Controller	Stuart Masheter
Executive Managing Editor	Adèle Hayward
Managing Art Editor	Nick Harris
Art Director	Peter Luff
Publisher	Stephanie Jackson

First American Edition, 2007

Published in the United States by DK Publishing,
375 Hudson Street, New York, New York 10014

07 08 09 10 11 10 9 8 7 6 5 4 3 2 1

ED251—September 2007

Published in the United Kingdom by Dorling
Kindersley Ltd.

A catalog record for this book is available from
the Library of Congress

ISBN: 978-0-7566-3170-3

DK books are available at special discounts when
purchased in bulk for sales promotions, premiums,
fund-raising, or educational use. For details, contact:
DK Publishing Special Markets, 375 Hudson
Street, New York, New York 10014 or
SpecialSales@dk.com.

Printed and bound in China by Leo Paper Group
Discover more at www.dk.com

Contents

1 Listening

2 Talking

Introduction

Communication is the heart and soul of management at absolutely every level. Without communication skills you can't express your thoughts, convince others, or negotiate. With good communication skills you can expect to win arguments, make sales, mediate, educate, inform, and even inspire.

There are no limits to the opportunities to practice and expand your communication skills, and now there is an ever-growing array of media to use to your advantage, as long as you know how. You'll probably need to start off by simply learning to be a better listener—if you can't see how listening is going to help you to state your case then you really do need to read *Effective Communications*. Good communication is a two-way process—the word itself comes from the idea of sharing or communing. What separates the good communicators from the truly great communicators is the ability to understand the messages of others and fine-tune or manipulate them so that they reinforce your own arguments when you are communicating

Good communication is key to success in life and in business

your message. You don't have to
be a speechmaker to be a great
communicator. You are making
statements even before you open
your mouth or put pen to paper,
so you should always compare the
signals you are sending out to
those you want to send.

Starting with the fundamental
skills of listening and talking, this
book considers all of the ways in which you send out
messages every day—from negotiating to email writing. It
looks at ways of making your point that use all the tools at
your disposal, whether that is voice, paper, video, or the
positioning of your own body. By reading it, and by taking
on board its armory of tips, techniques, and tactics, you will
learn more about what people are really saying, about how
to make others understand you, how to get agreement, and
how to achieve your goals.

Communication is management, so take the time to
learn how to make your words and gestures work better.
You, and your colleagues, will never regret the effort.

Assessing Your Skills

This quiz is designed to test your awareness of your own communication strengths and weaknesses, with an analysis of your results that will help you focus on weaker areas. Answer the questions as honestly as possible before and after reading the book—once to highlight areas where you need help, and the second time to see what you've learned.

Before   After

1 When other people are talking to you what are you most likely to do?

A Give them my full attention and remain silent.
B Listen, and repeat back to them what they just said.
C Start thinking about work I need to do.

2 What kind of questions do you ask?

A I don't ask any questions—my job is mainly to do whatever I'm told to do.
B I use open questions to get fuller answers.
C I get to the point, ask the tough questions, and get the real answers.

3 Where in the office do you mainly ask questions of others?

A I seek them out when they are in the corridors.
B I usually ask questions during meetings.
C I ask questions in the privacy of my office.

4 What is your relationship with your colleagues based on?

A We have a mutual and polite respect.
B On a complex web of social and cultural issues.
C On a well-defined hierarchy of job titles and roles.

Before   After

5 What would you do if there were a hidden agenda affecting workplace communication?

A I would avoid the subject—it makes life easier.
B I'd take it into account and consider if it might actually be based on fact.
C I'd tell those concerned to get over whatever the problem was and get on with the job.

6 Negotiating is about:

A Making compromises and giving in to others.
B Finding common ground for the parties to a dispute.
C Winning the battle and being proved right.

7 How do you feel when you have to say "No"?

A I find it one of the hardest things to do.
B It usually takes some forethought to get it right.
C I have no difficulty with it. No means no.

8 What do you think has the greatest effect on the language you use at work?

A Senior members of staff and corporate communications materials.
B My immediate colleagues, my friends outside work.
C I'm not aware of anything that has a particular effect on the language I use.

9 The main purpose of meetings is to:

A Give the appearance that everyone is doing something.
B Decide on a course of action to deal with a situation.
C Inform people of developments as they occur.

10 You have a presentation to do. What aids do you think you'll need?

A A big box of slides and a slide projector.
B I'll use whatever is available at the venue.
C Nothing extra, my PowerPoint presentations are already prepared and ready to go.

	Before	After

11 **How do you feel about people asking questions during your presentation?**

A I dread them—I might make a fool of myself.
B I don't mind—I'm ready and I have help at hand.
C I love them. I know my stuff and I like to share it.

12 **How do you prepare for a telephone call?**

A I take a deep breath before lifting the receiver.
B I compile a check list of what I want from the call.
C I just pick up the phone and dial the number.

13 **For you, email is best described as:**

A Much easier than having to phone people.
B My life—I don't know how I'd cope without it.
C A pest and a timewaster and better to ignore.

14 **Someone asks if you'd talk to the press about your team's project. You answer:**

A I'd rather do anything than talk to the press.
B Of course, but I'll need to ask the journalist some questions before we go ahead.
C I'd love to—all publicity is good publicity.

15 **If you have to fire someone, what do you do?**

A I get Human Resources to do it—it's their job.
B I do it face to face, but jointly with Human Resources.
C I do it myself, just to get it done and over with.

Final Scores

	A	B	C
Before			
After			

Analysis

Mostly As

You're more of a listener than a talker and may lack a certain amount of confidence when it comes to presenting yourself. Communications are something that happens to you at work, rather than something you see as an essential tool for your own progress. This may be due to factors such as your role in the hierarchy or personal shyness, but examine your answers carefully and ask yourself if you are avoiding issues, or subconsciously suggesting that your own ideas aren't worth pushing forward.

Mostly Bs

You understand that communications touches every part of business life and you try to prepare and plan so that your own messages are as clear and effective as possible. However, there's more to really effective communication than a thorough understanding of the techniques involved. If you haven't marked any Cs it could mean that you are a great mediator but hesitate to project your own message to others. That could be part of your role, but it could also mean that you feel you are more a conduit for information than a source of ideas or messages.

Mostly Cs

You are confident and forthright and probably feel very much at ease with the idea of presenting your own ideas. However, true communication is a two-way exchange of ideas. Your success in presenting your own messages may be blinding you to a tendency to ignore or fail to seek out the thoughts and attitudes of others. You might want to consider the techniques for encouraging feedback from others and incorporating their ideas and emotions into your own messages.

Conclusion

Having completed this analysis go ahead and read the book, bearing in mind any obvious facts that emerge from the above. Pay special attention to the areas highlighted by your responses as well as the tips and techniques—these will help you to reduce the number of As and achieve a more balanced mixture of Bs and Cs. When you've read the book, complete the quiz again and see where you have picked up techniques, tips, and attitudes toward communicating more effectively.

Listening 1

Communication is management. Whether your goal is to get others to agree, make yourself heard, instruct, motivate, or inspire, communication is key. Many, if not most, business problems spring from failure to communicate, leading to misunderstandings and mistrust. What's usually at fault is a failure to start out with the most important element in communication—listening. If you want to influence people, you first need to know how they think, and good listening is the building block for everything else in business. This chapter shows you how to:

- Listen actively to others
- Ask questions that count
- Identify hidden agendas
- Bridge communication gaps
- Clarify and confirm mixed messages

Be Heard by Listening Better

The word "communication" comes from the idea of sharing, or communing, with others. The truly great communicators know that good listening is one of the key weapons in their arsenal of techniques.

Improve Your Listening Skills

Great listening is what enables you to talk to people in their own terms, to build bridges, and to help people feel they are being heard and that what you are proposing is good for them as well as for you. However, nobody really teaches us to listen, any more than they teach us to breathe or run. It's a skill that we are presumed to have naturally, but some natural skills are better than others, and there is always room for improvement.

Learn to Listen

We can speak at a rate of over 100 words a minute, but we can listen at more than twice that speed. This means that there is often a temptation for our brains to be doing other things at the same time as listening. We may think or say that we are listening, but more

To understand you must first listen properly

often than not we are actually thinking our own thoughts, getting distracted, worrying, or daydreaming. Worst of all, we interrupt people when they are talking, or jump in and finish their sentences. Interruption suggests that you lack the time or the patience to hear someone out. This means that you will never really hear what that person is saying, and may be signaling to him that you don't think he is worth listening to. How rude is that?

> **We were given two ears and one mouth because listening is twice as hard as talking.**
>
> Traditional

Good Listening Techniques

There are techniques that you can employ to become a better listener immediately. Some of them require you to use your whole body, not just your ears and brain.

→ Make the person to whom you are listening your focus. Stop everything else that you are doing.

→ If you are listening to a group take your cell phone out and turn it off.

→ Face the person you are listening to; if necessary shift your body position.

→ Listen carefully to the words but don't be deaf to the emotion and feeling behind them. Strong words could be masking weak feelings and vice versa.

→ Be aware of prejudices and preconceptions that may influence your listening.

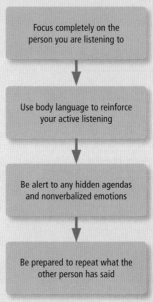

Focus completely on the person you are listening to

Use body language to reinforce your active listening

Be alert to any hidden agendas and nonverbalized emotions

Be prepared to repeat what the other person has said

→ Acknowledge and confirm the message by paraphrasing and repeating key points (knowing that you will be doing this is an effective way to help you to listen more attentively).

→ If it's appropriate to state your own views (and it may not be) then do this only after you have listened to what is being said.

Make sure that you maintain eye contact throughout. Don't just make eye contact while listening then break it off when you are speaking. Make it clear to those who want to talk to you that you have blocked off your time for their benefit. If you are likely to be called away, or to run out of time, make it clear before it happens.

Listen Actively

Active listening (sometimes referred to as empathetic listening) is a technique frequently used by educators and counselors because it is a structured technique of listening that focuses firmly on the person speaking.

Pay Attention

Active listening goes beyond passive listening (where you hear what is being said but don't respond). It encourages the speaker to voice his views and ensures that the listener has really understood what was meant. The key element of active listening is that, whether or not you agree with what's being said, you repeat it yourself by paraphrasing the key points. This serves a number of purposes:

- It encourages you to give the subject your full attention.
- It shows the speaker that you are paying attention.
- It reduces the possibility of misunderstandings.
- It helps present the listener in an empathetic light—trying to understand, not contradict.
- It encourages the speaker to develop aloud his argument and his feelings about it.

TECHNIQUES *to* practice

Paraphrasing may seem easy but it is actually quite a difficult skill to master. It's a good idea to practice before attempting to use the technique to clarify genuine problems. As a test, try to paraphrase a difficult communicator, perhaps a politician—political statements are rarely clear and concise.

- Read a short paragraph of text that has been written or spoken by a politician.
- Try to put it into clear language and read it back.
- Refine your words until you have produced a clear and succinct statement.
- Notice what your paraphrase reveals about how much or how little has really been said in the original statement.

Learn to Paraphrase

Paraphrasing is a crucial aspect of active listening because you would otherwise merely be repeating, parrot fashion, what the speaker said. It shows that you are listening to, and thinking about, what is being said.
Paraphrasing can:

- Introduce words or terms that can be used as tools to describe problems and clarify situations
- Encourage people to elaborate on something they want to define
- Subtly bring a new interpretation to a statement
- Eliminate potential confusion on an issue.

Active Listening

Listen carefully and attentively while maintaining eye contact

Acknowledge phrases or messages and repeat the key points

Say that you have understood the emotional or psychological impact

Allow the speaker to confirm or contradict your rephrasing

Take Notes

The ability to take accurate notes is an important addition to your listening skills. Well kept notes will allow you to clarify and reflect on what is said in meetings, and also provide a useful written record.

Keep a Clear Record

Very few meetings have a formal record keeper so you will be responsible for recording what was important for you. This will have a direct influence on how you act on points raised in the meeting, and will put you in a strong position at a later date if others ask where ideas came from. Taking notes not only shows that you are paying attention, but also provides you with a record of the meeting long after the event. It can sometimes be quite difficult to concentrate on what someone is saying when you are trying to make a note of previous remarks, so keep up with the meeting by using shorthand or other techniques.

Use Symbols

You might not be trained in shorthand but that doesn't have to stop you from using symbols and shortcuts to speed up your note taking. Some of the symbols below are taken from the field of science and others have been influenced by the shortcuts used by people when sending text messages on cell phones.

@	at	**bc**	because	**v**	very
no.	number	**tda**	today	**tt**	that
>	more than	**tmo**	tomorrow	**2**	too
<	less than	**yta**	yesterday	∴	therefore

Squares, triangles, circles, stars, or other symbols can be used to denote specific action points.

A system of notetaking developed for students attending lectures at Cornell University has proved very helpful for many people when attending meetings or briefings.

This is a dual system, with the advantage that your notes will serve not only as a full record of a meeting, but also as an memory aid of the more important points raised.

- Take a large notebook and prepare it by drawing a vertical line down the page, 2½ in (6 cm) in from the left, making a wide margin.
- Take notes in the area on the right-hand side of the margin, using the margin area as your "recall" column.
- When the meeting is over, summarize the key words or action points of each stage of the meeting and write them down in the recall margin.

Write It Down

Although there are many note-taking devices—such as dictaphones, PDAs, laptop computers, and automatic voice recorders—most people still reach for pen and paper when they need to take notes during a meeting or conference. Your listening skills will be reflected in how efficiently you can transfer the important points of what is being said to paper, and how useful your paper record is after the event. If your handwriting is not very legible, transcribe your notes into a fair copy or on to your computer as soon as possible after you've taken them down—your memory of the detail of what was said will soon fade and, as time passes, it will become increasingly difficult to make sense of what you have written down.

TIP If you decide to use your own symbols or system of shorthand, write out a key to the symbols somewhere on your notes.

Avoid Preconceptions

Whether or not you are aware of it, you always see other people through a filter of preformed ideas. Preconceived impressions of people affect how you respond to what they say.

Build Good Relationships

We usually think of "relationships" in terms of the people we know and talk to. In your social life you will probably mix with people like yourself, from a similar background and with similar values or interests. You can't choose your colleagues at work, and will have to rely on your people skills to ensure that you get on well with them and can communicate effectively.

Change the Environment
Getting your team together occasionally in a less formal environment can often help to improve relationships at work.

Factors that Affect Relationships

There are a number of factors that will influence the way you perceive others and the way they perceive you. Consider whether any of the following affect how you listen to colleagues and how they listen to you.

If you think any of these factors is causing a communication problem, ask people informally how they see that aspect of you.

→ **Status**—While you may have a more senior title, the person you are speaking to may see himself as an expert in the field.

→ **Socioeconomic sensitivity**—It is always best to be sensitive to the different financial circumstances of others.

→ **Race and culture**—Embracing diversity in the workplace makes the work environment comfortable for everyone.

→ **Age**—Age is just a number; look at performance, not age.

→ **Gender**—Don't fall prey to preconceptions such as "Men are more goal oriented" and "Women excell at multitasking."

→ **Work skills/discipline**—Those qualified in some disciplines may believe they have a status higher than their job title.

→ **Known background**—A reputation will follow you wherever you go. Try to find out what yours is—you may be surprised.

→ **Education**—Different positions require different levels of education and skill; recognize and appreciate these differences.

→ **Wealth**—You may not consider yourself rich, but others may.

Examples of Nonjudgmental Statements

HIGH IMPACT

- He'll bring a lot of knowledge and experience to the team
- She'll probably have very strong communication skills that will be an asset to the team
- His technical skills are superb—that's what we pay for
- Our policy of diverse ethnicity attracts the best people

NEGATIVE IMPACT

- He's too old to have anything useful left to offer
- She'll be too much of a distraction for the male team members
- His scruffiness will give a bad impression of the organization
- Foreigners won't understand our values

Ask the Questions that Matter

If you want to know something you have to ask, but the way in which you ask will affect the answer you get. Asking questions is a skill that few people are trained in, yet it is essential to good listening.

Learn How to Ask Questions

Better questions get better answers, so choose your questions with care and try to put people at ease so that they will give good answers. When people are relaxed they will be more inclined to provide more information. If you behave like an interrogator you will make people nervous and less likely to give detailed answers. Ask one question at a time and wait for the answer before asking another question. If you ask too many questions at once you will get partial answers and important facts may be glossed over or ignored. Use the active listening technique to show your interest and to help you to focus on the answer.

TECHNIQUES *to* practice

Before you ask any questions it is important to prepare them properly. What you ask will have an impact on what you learn, so start by asking yourself exactly what it is you need to find out.

- Check if you need a specific piece of information about an event that has happened or something that's going to happen in the future.
- If you are new to a subject, determine what you will need to find out about it before you start asking questions.
- If you need the opinion or perspective of someone else make sure you approach them to ask for their input.
- If someone needs your help with something find out what exactly they need to know.
- Choose your questions carefully and, if necessary, make a note of them, checking them off so that you don't get distracted and forget to ask something you need to know.

Give Reasons for Your Questions

Get the Full Picture If you allow people to speak until they've finished, without interrupting them, you're far more likely to hear a full account of a situation or event.

Let people know why you are asking questions. This is particularly important if you are to avoid a defensive reaction when you're asking people about themselves or their work. You could start by putting the questions in a context—"I'm here to look at ways in which the organization can improve performance. Do you and your team have any suggestions on how we can reduce the number of nonproductive tasks?"

Wait for an Answer

Don't fall into the trap of answering your own questions. When you already have an idea of what the answers might be, it is easy to suggest answers—"Do you think the meetings are losing their focus because there are too many people in attendance?" This may give the impression that you are uninterested in the opinions of others.

TIP If you think you already know the answer to a question, you will ask questions that confirm that view. Ask more questions that will find another angle.

Use Different Types of Question

Tailor your question to suit the circumstances. There are

Seize the Moment You can ask questions anywhere, not just in meetings. Take advantage of chance, informal encounters.

many different types of question, and the one you choose to ask in a particular situation will determine the type and quality of the information you receive.

- **Closed question**—This only allows for a "yes" or "no" answer: "Did you finish that report last Friday?"
- **Open question**—This encourages the person being questioned to volunteer information: "What reports have you been working on recently?"
- **Follow-up question/Drilling down**—This technique uses the answer to a question to form another question that asks for more detail: "You say you are unhappy with the team project. Is that because of the project, or is it because of the team?"
- **What if? question**—This is an open question that encourages speculation: "What if you were the regional manager? What would you change?"

> **Quality questions create a quality life. Successful people ask better questions, and as a result, they get better answers.**
>
> Anthony Robbins

- **Leading question**—This leads toward a certain answer: "Do you think the new shift structure breaches the regulations, or can we get away with it?"

You will often get a better answer if you introduce your question before asking it. If a question deals with an important, delicate, or complicated issue then say so before you ask. Preface a difficult question with "I realize this is a difficult question to answer, so take your time." This approach will be much more likely to generate a considered response than firing off difficult questions without an introduction, which will often put people on the defensive and make them reluctant to give you the information you need.

CASE study: Choosing Your Moment

John, a regional manager, was sent to find out why a local branch was underperforming. He interviewed the people concerned and announced that he was satisfied with what he had heard, even though he was fairly sure there was more to the problem than he was being told. He then prepared to leave while making small talk about sports. As the branch manager walked him to the elevator, he added casually, "By the way, why aren't you getting along with your salesman?" The answer was far more honest than anything John had heard in the interview room. By listening as carefully to what hadn't been said as he did to what had, John found the clue he needed to correct the problem.

- *By using a technique that relies on the fact that people are more likely to give a full answer if they are relaxed, John was able to get to the root of the problem.*
- *He was able to deal with the situation before it had an adverse effect on the branch's accounting.*

Confirm and Clarify

Avoiding misunderstandings requires more than simply asking questions and listening to the answers. You must also clarify that what you think you have heard is, in fact, what the other person meant you to hear.

Establish What You Want

Ask yourself exactly what it is you want to gain from a conversation, asking people questions, or calling a meeting. If someone else has initiated the communication, whether it is a chat over coffee or a one-to-one meeting, ask yourself what his objective was. If you are not sure of his objective after the meeting, then it is possible either that he didn't have one or that you missed it. Ask, but do so tactfully unless you want to suggest that he has a hidden agenda. If you think that someone is trying to air a problem or gain support ask him gently if he is telling you something because he wants to hear your opinion, or because he expects you to do something.

Clarity is the key to finding the solution to a problem

TECHNIQUES *to* practice

Lack of clarity about an issue can often lead to misunderstandings and poor decision making.
In order to clarify the message you should repeat the key points that have been made in simple terms, making a deliberate effort to remove any ambiguity from the message.

- Summarize the points made.
- Get the other person's agreement that your summary is a correct one.
- Separate the points that relate to the problem, and those that relate to the solution.
- Agree on the action each one of you will take—even if that means taking no action at all.

Make the Right Diagnosis

In the same way that a doctor diagnoses an illness, the good manager has to distinguish between the problem itself and the symptoms of that problem.

→ Begin by making clear what the goal of the project or action was, and state which aspect of it hasn't worked.
→ Don't simply accept that it's gone wrong—find out exactly what has failed or is failing.
→ Ask everyone concerned for their opinion on the problem.
→ Then make your own judgment before deciding what can be done to deal with the problem.

Define the Problem and Find the Solution

Once an objective is made clear the next step is to separate the two key areas of discussion—the problem and the solution. Unless someone just wants to vent his anger by talking about his problems, it is always more productive to define the problem and then move the focus on to the solution. Ask clarifying questions—they will not only ensure that you have understood, but also help the other person to examine and crystallize his own thoughts. Asking exactly "when," "who," "how," "where," and "why" works wonders when it comes to clearing up misconceptions. Watch out for assumptions—if the problems involve deadlines, numbers, or complaints, then make sure that there is agreement on precise dates and figures and specific complaints. Many problems arise simply because one person has misunderstood what another means.

> **Executives who get there and stay suggest solutions when they present the problems.**
> Malcolm S. Forbes

Be Aware of Hidden Agendas

Sometimes, careful questions and attentive listening just aren't enough to lead to a complete understanding of a situation. Hidden agendas are those unspoken factors that shape actions and understanding and can be difficult to overcome because you are unaware of their existence. If you think that your messages are crystal clear, and others agree yet still don't pay attention to them, you should look for anything that may be acting as an obstacle. Try to identify what it is that may be interfering with communication. Factors worth considering are: covering up failure; saving face; personal ambition; pet ideas; preserving the future of a job, a team, or a department; cultural gaps; prejudice; personal ties or associations.

Deal with the Problem

You will need to deal with these factors with extreme tact and you should always be aware that you too may be influenced by some of them. If you think there is a communication gap of any type then try to find a hidden cause. When you

Confronting the Problem If you believe someone has a hidden agenda, raise the subject in private.

CASE study: Understanding the Culture

Wayne was recruited to head a new department in an organization based abroad. One of the first steps he took was to introduce brainstorming sessions. This had been very successful for him previously, generating ideas, helping to bring colleagues together, and fostering a spirit of openness. Now, however, nobody suggested anything during the sessions and there was a lot of uncomfortable silence. Unwilling to accept that his new team couldn't produce a single idea, Wayne tackled each person individually. He discovered that the culture of both the organization and the country in which he was working was based on a strong respect for hierarchy. The senior management was not happy discussing strategy and change in front of junior staff, and the junior staff was uncomfortable about speaking when senior management members were present.

• *Wayne quickly realized that he would discover the cause of the problem only by discussing the situation individually with members of his team.*

• *As a result of what he learned about the local and organizational culture, he decided to break down the brainstorming sessions into small groups of peers and had significant success.*

have identified one, discuss the issue with those concerned, taking steps to prevent the conversation becoming confrontational. Once you have identified a hidden agenda, do your best to persuade the individual concerned to acknowledge it. Once a hidden agenda has been brought out into the open it is much easier to deal with. However, uncovering an agenda may require considerable diplomacy, depending on the individual's reason for concealing his motives. Consider carefully whether the agenda needs to be revisited, or whether you can live with the situation as it is. For example, if it becomes clear that a member of your team is worried about losing his influence, you can find a way to reassure him and to help him to achieve his goals while he is on the way to meeting your objectives.

Talking 2

Talking is the most personal, direct, and forceful way in which you communicate every day. The way you talk has the greatest impact on how other people interact with you and yet it is a skill that is commonly taken for granted or only partially understood. To make sure that you really say something when you talk this chapter will explain:

• How to communicate with people using body language and nonverbal signals
• Techniques for expressing yourself better
• How to negotiate successfully
• Techniques for winning arguments

Learn to Use Body Language

A great deal of what people understand when someone talks is what they are told by voice tone, expression, and body language. Your nonverbal language may be communicating more clearly than your voice.

Believe Your Eyes

Dr. Albert Mehrabian, a leading authority in nonverbal communication, concluded that of the three elements in face-to-face communication—words, tone of voice, and body language—words could account for as little as seven per cent of meaning, tone of voice 38 percent, and body language 55 percent. If you want to inform, negotiate, or win arguments then you will need to communicate with your eyes and be careful about the signals you are sending out to other people.

Read Nonverbal Signals

Nonverbal communication includes facial expression, gesture, tone of voice, speed of speech, how you hold your body, and where you position yourself in relation to others. Nonverbal signals are often strong enough to override the meaning of words. Unnatural eye contact and confrontational body positions send out very disturbing messages. Similarly, someone who won't meet your eyes while speaking is sending out a strong signal that what she is saying is not what she really feels. However, be aware that body language can be affected by emotions and "come out all wrong", just as verbal language does. Just because someone is unable to meet your eyes when speaking to you doesn't mean that she is lying or hiding something— it could mean simply that she is shy, embarrassed, or even nervous about your reaction to what she is telling you.

Your body language speaks volumes

What Your Gestures Say About You

We unconsciously assign specific meanings to particular gestures made while someone is speaking. Your message may be positive, but your body language says otherwise.

Make Eye Contact Eye contact suggests honesty and openness, but only if maintained for a couple of seconds; if you hold it for longer than that it will become intrusive and confrontational.

Think of Your Body Adopting "closed" body language, such as folding your arms or crossing your legs away from the person who is speaking, may suggest that you are protecting yourself or blocking out what is being said to you.

Watch Your Signals Many people touch their ears out of habit, but you need to be aware of the message you are sending, particularly when you touch or pull at your earlobe—this suggests that you have doubts about what is being said.

Emotional Intelligence (EQ) and Body Language

In his book, *Emotional Intelligence*, Daniel Goleman popularized the belief that there are five emotional "competencies," or skills. The starting point is knowing your own emotions, so you can then manage them, and motivate yourself to use them. The next step is to recognize and understand the emotions of others, so you can manage the relationship and interact with them more effectively.

The Five Emotional Skills

Being aware of your emotions

⇩

Learning to control your emotions

⇩

Assessing the emotions of others

⇩

Picking up clues from body language

⇩

Relating successfully with others

Manage Your Emotions

Goleman believes that in order to get to the fifth skill, which is key to communicating in business, you need to have mastered the other four. Take a moment to examine your emotions before talking to others. Are you intimidated, afraid, angry, or resentful? If you don't manage those emotions they will interfere with your ability

Motivated Body Language

HIGH IMPACT

- Sitting forward or leaning toward the speaker
- Standing erect if not seated
- Placing hands on hips
- Opening eyes wide
- Making animated hand gestures

NEGATIVE IMPACT

- Avoiding eye contact
- Turning toward the exit
- Checking the time frequently
- Folding arms across the chest
- Scratching the back of the neck
- Looking downward

> **You can read somebody's attitude—you can spot that in their body language, their eye contact.**
>
> Camille Lavington

to motivate yourself and others. They will influence the way you address people and could cause a communication problem. Emotions are often conveyed more effectively through nonverbal communication than through speech, so consider how people's body language may be sending out clues about how they're feeling. The cause of their frustration, nerves, or boredom may not even be you, but since you are the person hoping to convince them it is up to you to try to remove any barriers to your communication with them. If people seem to be alert and animated at the beginning of your argument, but are soon conveying lack of interest, you will need to change your approach halfway through in order to win them back.

CASE study: Respecting Personal Space

John, an advertising salesman for a magazine publisher, was perceived as aggressive and even bullying by the members of his team, even though he never shouted and was always respectful of other people's points of view. He was mystified by his team's negative reaction whenever he spoke to them, and he eventually sought the advice of his colleague, Ahmed. Ahmed pointed out to John that he would position himself slightly closer to others when he spoke, thereby encroaching on their sense of personal space and suggesting a combative attitude. John took this criticism to heart and began to stand a little farther back when he was speaking to people.

• *By taking some timely advice from his colleague, John was able to improve his body language.*
• *His new body language meant that the members of his team felt more relaxed when he was speaking to them. They became more open to his ideas, and their performance improved.*

Express Yourself

It may sometimes seem that other people express themselves so much better and so much more memorably than you do. However, there are several things you can do to improve the power of your words.

Make Every Word Count

For the really good communicator there is no such thing as idle chat. Every exchange serves a purpose, whether it's cementing a friendship, conveying a vision, or persuading others. Some people are naturally gifted with their ability to express themselves, but even if you don't have a way with words you can improve your expression considerably by:

- Choosing your words carefully
- Keeping it clear and concise
- Making it real
- Appealing to the senses
- Telling the whole story.

The right language will get your point across

Choose Your Words Carefully

Unless you have a talent for spontaneous speech, think about what you want to say before you are called upon to say it. Choose language that matches your audience. Too

Jargon-Free Language

HIGH IMPACT	NEGATIVE IMPACT
• We are creating something completely new	• The organization is facing a paradigm shift
• We provide cheap phone calls for organizations	• We're big players in the B2BVoIP/PSTN arena
• We have a policy of internal promotion so that people can plan their careers	• We are good at leveraging the human resources at our disposal in this organization
• Our emphasis is on selling to our largest market	• We're concentrating our efforts on marketizing

many business people use elaborate language, thinking it sounds better. It doesn't, it just sounds more corporate. Practise your speech aloud, and imagine that you are talking to friends. Are you using words you normally use? Could you make your point using simpler words?

Make It Real

Make it easy for people to understand what you're talking about. Make it real by making reference to real world experiences, creating scenarios, and utilizing simile and metaphor to get your point across.

- Use examples from the real world to remind people of their experience or to explain how what you are saying has affected someone—"Remember how you felt the last time the job description was changed."
- Create a scenario to illustrate your point—"If we started to sell these on-line, we would save a fortune on the cost of running retail outlets."
- Use simile and metaphor to demonstrate a point concretely by comparing something to something else.

TIP **Think how you would explain an issue to someone with no experience of your subject. If you can make it clear to him it should be clear to everyone.**

Appeal to the Senses

We interpret the world through our physical senses of touch, taste, smell, sight, and hearing. Referring to the senses makes what you are saying more immediate and real. This is true even when talking about abstract ideas such as emotions. We might talk about the "feel" of a proposal, or whether it "smells" good. Describing ideas in terms of the senses can add impact to what you say. Neurolinguistic Programming (NLP) recognizes that the way individuals speak and behave is directly linked to the senses that are most important to them. For example, someone who is very visually oriented will respond better to phrases such as "I see what you mean" and "It looks that way to me", while someone who is more hearing oriented is more likely to respond to an auditory statement, such as "I hear what you're saying."

CASE study: Sharing Your Feelings

David's co-worker Sam wasn't carrying her share of their workload. When David confronted her with this Sam became defensive and withdrawn. He decided to try again. He started by saying, "Every month I see the reports to be done piling up on my desk." Then he said how he felt about this: "My heart sinks and I get a bit panicky about it." He explained why that was the case: "I feel that it's not fair, and I worry that because I'm spending more time on administration my creative work is suffering and it will affect my prospects." He then pointed out the outcome he wanted: "What I'd really like is for us to divide these jobs equally, with each of us taking responsibility for the task." Sam considered what David had said and realized that she had been acting unfairly. Soon she was doing her fair share.

• *Because David changed his approach to Sam and invited her to share his feelings and thinking, she was more open to seeing the situation from his point of view.*
• *Their new co-operation meant that they were able to get through their workload quickly and efficiently.*

Think Before You Speak

Rather than bluntly delivering an observation, request, or command, think about what it is that you want to achieve. How you phrase your words will affect the response you receive to what you have said.

→ Think about what you are responding to and state the facts.
→ Think about how you feel about this.
→ Consider what it is that causes this feeling.
→ Think about what outcome you want.

Be Honest with Yourself

While it is acceptable to talk about your "passion" for business, almost any other feeling is considered suspect. Even admitting to having emotions sometimes seems like weakness, so people often refuse to acknowledge feelings such as insecurity, jealousy, or nervousness. Take a good look at your reaction to events, challenges, and other people, and be sure that you are being honest with yourself about the nature and depth of your emotions.

Tell the Whole Story

Taking account of feelings can make our observations much more compelling and persuade others to act on our suggestions. By including information about what we feel, and what we want, when we make statements, we can recreate that feeling in the minds of the people we're talking to. That, in turn, makes it much more likely that agreement and a satisfactory outcome will eventually be achieved.

> **Difficulty in managing relationships sabotages more business than anything else.**
>
> John Kotter

Learn to Negotiate

We negotiate all the time with those around us—with our friends, partners, children, and work colleagues. Negotiation takes place every time two or more people need to agree on something.

Understand Negotiation

Negotiation is about coming to an agreement in which everyone involved gets what they want. Remember that the goal of any negotiation is not that one side will win or the other side will lose, but about reaching a solution that is acceptable to all the parties involved in the process. Start off any negotiation by asking everyone concerned to confirm that their goal is simply to reach an agreement, not to win. At the heart of negotiation lies the distinction between your "needs", on which you cannot compromise, and your "interests", on which you can. The more serious the needs and interests the more delicate the negotiation, but the principle remains the same. The first step is to think through and identify your situation, your needs, and your interests. The second step is to make sure that the other party has done the same.

think SMART

A lot of the real business of negotiation takes place away from the negotiating table. Issues of reputation and saving face can get in the way when people sit down together for formal talks.

Try to have an informal meeting before the negotiation itself. This is a great time to build bridges, drop hints about what you can and can't do without, and encourage others to do the same. It often helps to call a "time out" or coffee break in the middle of a negotiation, so that people can relax a little and speak to each other in a less formal environment.

Learn Basic Negotiation Tactics

Consider the alternative to

Reaching a Solution The goal of any negotiation is not to win but to reach a solution that suits everyone.

a negotiated agreement. If it is unacceptable, follow this process to reach agreement:

- Separate the people from the problem—make it clear that it is everyone versus the problem, not each person pitted against the other.
- Emphasize fairness—if you make it clear that fairness is top of the list you will find others more likely to buy into the negotiation and be constructive.
- Separate your interests from your needs—be honest with yourself about what is important and what you are prepared to compromise on.
- Don't just think about what you need, think about what you can concede.
- Make provision for others to save face—if the end result is even slightly humiliating to any of the parties involved, or if there is the faintest suspicion of unfairness, this will work against you, and will almost certainly ensure that the agreement will not endure.

Say "No" When You Need To

In an ideal world, negotiation would lead to unanimous agreement on all issues. In the real world, however, there are times when your only option is to refuse. Saying "no", however, is rarely easy. You may be unwilling to offend the person making the request, or you may think that a refusal makes it look as if you're incapable of doing what is being asked of you. You may even be worried that you won't be asked again, or afraid that a refusal will mean that you'll be unpopular with your colleagues.

Learn to Push Back

It is vital to learn to say "no". The inability to do so can have several negative outcomes.

- If you believe that you should have said "no" you may feel resentful toward the requester.
- Others may make assumptions about your willingness to do things when asked.
- You may be perceived as being weak and malleable.
- You will probably become stressed by your workload.

> One of the most powerful words is "No"

Avoid dwelling on your refusal—someone who needs help badly will simply look for it elsewhere.

The Way that You Say It

"No" is a little word with a lot of power behind it, and this is the reason that most people find it difficult to say when someone asks them to do something. However, reasonable people will usually find a refusal much more acceptable if it is accompanied by a good reason. It can be a good idea to show that you understand the requester's needs. You could say, "I'm sorry, I know the workload you're dealing with but I just can't help today." The "no" still stands, but you have softened the message by suggesting you are aware of the needs of the person making the request.

Reinforce Your Message

If you end up doing things that you have refused to do then you are not saying "no" sufficiently effectively. If you want to emphasize your refusal to do something without seeming rude or obstructive, try the following:

→ Don't smile—a smile will weaken your message.

→ Don't ask any further questions, such as "How much?" or "By when?" This suggests that you are open to persuasion.

→ Stand up if someone standing asks you to do something. Mirroring body language shows that you are identifying with the person making the request.

→ Say "no" earlier rather than later. Apologize for interrupting and get your "no" in quickly.

→ Pre-empt a request by apologizing in advance, but making it clear that you are unavailable for that task.

→ Show that you are being reasonable by offering alternatives. "I can't do that for you today, but I have some free time next week" will make you seem helpful even as you refuse.

→ Remember that a "no" can be a prelude to negotiation. "I can't do that for you today, but I could do it next week if you were to help me with my report" opens up a whole range of possibilities.

Refuse with Confidence With body language to mirror the message, the refusal here is unequivocal.

Convey Conviction

Belief is inspiring. If you believe strongly in something you're more likely to influence others if you can clearly convey the strength of your feeling.

Don't Mix Your Message

Just as it is possible to end up doing what you refused to do, it is also possible to say "yes" and not be believed. The problem of mixed or unclear messages can make your fervent belief in something seem weak, unconvincing, or even fake. This is why you need to be able to convey your conviction. There are several ways of showing that you say what you mean, and you mean what you say.

- **Prepare to be spontaneous**

  If you have an opinion or belief that matters to you, you should be prepared to express it clearly. Passion alone won't carry the day, and your urgency will probably cause your words to trip over each other. Prepare for how you will say what it is you care about, so that it will be convincing.

  Choose Your Words You may not have a lot of time to speak, so make your point clearly and precisely.

CASE study: Recruiting Like Minds

Whenever Aisha pitched her ideas in a sales meeting there was general interest, but she always failed to get approval. This would leave her frustrated and unsure about her next move. She realized that because she felt uncomfortable speaking to a group her nervous body language made her look unsure of her argument. She identified key players in the audience and approached them individually to recruit them to her cause. By taking this approach Aisha won more general support, and when she raised the proposal at the next meeting it was approved by a majority.

• *Aisha's recognition that she displayed negative body language in situations where she felt uncomfortable meant that she was able to find a workable solution to her problem.*
• *Knowing that she had the support of colleagues gave her more confidence whenever she had to make a presentation to her colleagues during a meeting.*

- **Be succinct**
  The 60-second sales pitch and the business plan written on the back of a business card aren't signs of being rushed; they are signs that indicate that someone has taken the time and effort to distil thoughts to an absolute minimum. Being succinct is something you need to be able to do if you want to convince others.
- **Speak with your body**
  The body language of belief is unmistakable. There is a lot of eye contact, and strong hand gestures such as palms facing outward, fingers pressed together, or even a fist "punched" into the palm. Looking down, failing to make eye contact, and fiddling with your hands will all undermine your power to convince.

TIP When you are addressing a group speak firmly, slowly, and at your normal pitch—otherwise you will sound as if you're not in control.

Learn to Win Arguments

It pays to choose your battles carefully, but once you have decided that you are going to argue your case you must do everything you can to increase your chance of reaching the conclusion you want.

What Do You Want to Achieve?

Before you get into an argument make sure that you know exactly what you want to get out of it. You may want to:

- Clarify an issue
- Make a point
- Influence the actions of others
- Challenge assumptions
- Promote your strengths
- Clear the air.

Avoid using argument in inappropriate situations

However, if you want to settle a grudge, clear the air with someone with whom you clash, let off steam, or draw attention to someone's shortcomings, an argument is not the best option. There are other ways to figure out such situations.

Choose Your Battles

You can't win every argument, so begin by deciding whether you should argue at all, or whether there is another way to make your point. If you do need to argue a point, choose your time and place carefully. You will argue better on home (or at least neutral) ground. This means avoiding having an argument in someone else's office. If such a situation arises, say that you need to check your facts before proceeding and fix a time and place that will give you a better chance of succeeding in making your point reasonably and convincingly.

TIP Make it clear you're thinking of, and speaking for, others as well as yourself. The word "we" carries a lot more weight than "I."

Maximize Your Chance of Success

If you have a clear goal, certain approaches to an argument will increase your chance of success.

→ Make sure you know your subject and have facts and figures to hand to back up any premises you intend to introduce.

→ Know who you will be arguing against—personalities and reputations go a long way.

→ Pick your moment. If you choose a bad time, you increase the chance that bad temper will intrude.

→ Use techniques of active listening and follow up with questions to confirm the other person's point of view.

→ Separate the issues of problem and possible solution. Perhaps the argument could still become a negotiation after all.

→ Question generalizations. A lot of poor arguments break down when assumptions are challenged.

→ Summarize frequently. It helps you to gather your thoughts, keeps arguments moving at a reasonable pace, and focuses on the issues at stake and the likely outcome.

→ Don't get bogged down by a mistake. If the other person points out that one of your statements is wrong, accept the fact graciously and move on.

→ Don't make it personal. Try to focus on the problem or issue; don't attack individuals.

Effective Approaches to Arguments

HIGH IMPACT	**NEGATIVE IMPACT**
• Making simple points that everyone agrees on	• Using obscene language or being rude
• Using clear, unambiguous language	• Using pseudo-legal language
• Focusing on the issues involved rather than the people	• Blaming individuals and attacking people verbally
• Being understanding of the views of others	• Failing to acknowledge the point of view of other parties to the argument

Argue Logically

Sometimes you will have to present your case to people who hold conflicting or directly opposing views. It will pay to be able to construct a logical argument.

Learn to Be Logical

You present an argument by taking a position and defending it, often against a conflicting view. One of the most powerful ways of constructing compelling cases is through the process of logical argument. Logical arguments consist of a series of statements that combine to establish a conclusion by introducing the premise of the argument, and drawing an inference that can lead to only one conclusion. Logical argument improves with practice and, used well, will

The Logical Process

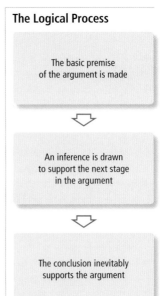

The basic premise of the argument is made

⇩

An inference is drawn to support the next stage in the argument

⇩

The conclusion inevitably supports the argument

think SMART

If you are going to construct a logical argument to support your case, it's best to draw it out first on paper, writing each premise in a box and setting down the links between the premises.

Before you present your argument take out this "mind map" and memorize the premises. This will help you remember your argument and deliver it with conviction. Make sure that the premises lead logically to the conclusion you need.

Stepping Toward the Conclusion

In any argument, the conclusion is the point that you want the other person to concede or acknowledge in order to establish that you have agreed. The premise and inference are ways of leading her to that conclusion.

→ The premise is a core assumption, a starting point on the way to the conclusion. It is introduced in a way that invites the other person to agree: "We both know that David doesn't have a business degree, and only MBAs get appointed to the board of this organization."
→ Once the premise has been agreed the next step is the inference, where you use the premise to arrive at a new statement: "So, as only MBAs get on to the board, David can forget about being appointed to the board."
→ If the other person accepts this new conclusion, then it becomes a premise and the argument moves on: "With David unable to get a board post it seems likely he will leave."

enable you to win most of your arguments. The strength of this approach is that the other person is asked to accept each stage at a time on what is really a journey toward the conclusion you already have in mind. The potential weakness of the process is that the more stages you introduce, the more links there will be. This can be hard to follow and any link, if challenged, could bring down the entire argument. Try to overcome this difficulty by keeping your arguments simple and to the point.

TIP Avoid introducing a premise with the word "obviously." This implies agreement rather than inviting it and can sound bullying.

Summary: Learning to Talk

There's a big difference between talking and making yourself understood. The best talkers know the value of listening as a tool to make their own arguments more compelling while at the same time making their audience more receptive. Great communication isn't about making yourself sound good, it's about making your message clear.

Getting the Message Across

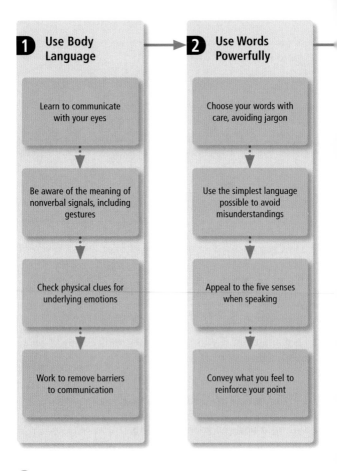

1 Use Body Language

Learn to communicate with your eyes

Be aware of the meaning of nonverbal signals, including gestures

Check physical clues for underlying emotions

Work to remove barriers to communication

2 Use Words Powerfully

Choose your words with care, avoiding jargon

Use the simplest language possible to avoid misunderstandings

Appeal to the five senses when speaking

Convey what you feel to reinforce your point

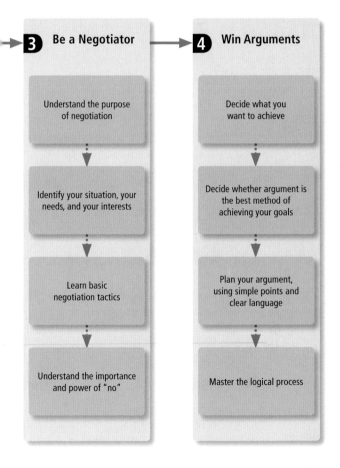

3 Be a Negotiator

Understand the purpose of negotiation

Identify your situation, your needs, and your interests

Learn basic negotiation tactics

Understand the importance and power of "no"

4 Win Arguments

Decide what you want to achieve

Decide whether argument is the best method of achieving your goals

Plan your argument, using simple points and clear language

Master the logical process

3

Talking to Groups

If you ask a group of business people what it is they are most afraid of, top of the list will be speaking in public. Talking in front of our peers is an essential people skill and a great management opportunity that should be seized, not shied away from. This chapter will show you how to:

• Impress during an interview
• Give first-class talks to your team
• Run meetings that matter
• Deliver memorable presentations
• Use presentation aids with confidence
• Become an effective public speaker

Impress at Interviews

The many books available on likely interview questions revolve around a handful of basics. If you practice answering those basic questions you will give a good account of yourself on the day of your interview.

5 minute FIX

If you're called to an internal interview at very short notice, take a few minutes to prepare yourself.

- Check your general appearance—you'll feel more confident if you look good.
- Write down a dozen likely questions and prepare answers to all of them.
- Take slow, deep breaths for a minute to calm yourself.

Know What to Say and How to Say It

Communicating in an interview should be easy—we all like to talk about ourselves. However, nervousness usually gets in the way. You can help yourself to overcome your nervousness by practicing your answers to likely questions in a mock interview with a friend. If you know just what to say, how to sit, and what you want to ask, you will feel confident. An interview is your opportunity to talk about yourself. This is one occasion where you can be sure that the person asking questions really does want to listen to your answers. Speak slowly, never faster than the person asking the question. Try to concentrate on what you are being asked, rather than on how nervous or uncertain you feel. If you don't understand a question, ask the interviewer to rephrase it—this is a better option than getting off the subject. And remember, while you may be anxious to get the job, the person interviewing you is just as anxious to find the right person.

TIP No matter how casual the organization, your appearance will be scrutinized. Dress appropriately and show that you have made an effort.

Practice Makes Perfect

In any job interview, certain questions are guaranteed to come up. Practice answering these questions so that you will appear confident and in control when you are faced with them during an interview.

→ **Why do you want this job?**
   This is where you will stress the areas where you think you provide a match for the job. Talk about how your skills suit the job rather than what the job is going to give you.

→ **Why do you want to work for this organization?**
   Do your research so that you can talk about the organization's dynamism, reputation, management style, and track record.

→ **What qualities do you think the job requires?**
   Draw attention to your strengths by listing the skills you can bring to the job.

→ **What can you contribute?**
   Give an example of something that shows how good you are, and say how the organization could benefit from this talent.

→ **What are your weak points?**
   This is a difficult question but you should never answer that you have none. Think about a weakness that you have overcome and turn the question around to show that you have the self-awareness, capacity, and will to improve.

Effective Interview Techniques

HIGH IMPACT

- Asking questions about the interviewer's experience of working for the organization
- Asking about opportunities and chances to develop your proposed role
- Asking questions based on research into the organization and its activities

NEGATIVE IMPACT

- Being passive—answering what you're asked without asking any questions
- Asking only about salary, conditions, and benefits
- Failing to find out anything before the interview about the organization's background, needs, or likely ambitions

The Group Interview

The least formidable type of interview is the one-to-one situation. Group interviews are utilized increasingly and you need to be aware of how to handle yourself with confidence in these situations if you are to give the best possible account of yourself.

Do Yourself Justice

Group interviews allow interviewers to watch how you interact with others—they will be trying to establish whether you are a leader, a follower, a bully, or are too shy to express yourself in a group. This type of interview usually involves a group exercise, a debate on which the participants have to reach an agreement, or a mock meeting that each person takes turns chairing. Don't try to be someone you are not, and don't allow the situation to stifle your expression. If you seem self-conscious and shy then the interviewer will suspect that you may have problems working in a team. Try to lead rather than follow, but do this in such a way that you demonstrate clearly to the interviewer that you are a team player.

Interviewers read every signal you send out

The Panel Interview

At a panel interview several people will be asking the questions. Most interviewees will find this very stressful and your ability to handle stress well will be one of the factors being examined by the panel. Make sure that you engage every member of the interview panel, making eye contact with those who don't actually speak—remember that they are just as much part of your audience as the person asking the question. Start by looking straight at the person who asks a question, then make eye contact with everyone on the panel as you talk, returning to the questioner as you finish making your response.

Clear and Confident Body language

Resist excited gestures, remember to look straight ahead but don't overdo the eye contact, and avoid "closed" body positions such as folded arms and crossed legs.

Make an Impression
Try to keep your expression friendly, but neutral. Practice some expressions in front of a mirror before an interview—you may be surprised by how some of them make you look.

Direct Your Gaze
Always look straight ahead, and keep your expression open, when meeting people for the first time. Avoid looking over people's heads—this will convey feelings of superiority.

Look Confident Stand up straight and keep your hands relaxed by your sides, ready to shake hands with your interviewers. Putting your hands in your pockets will look too casual for the situation.

Share the Message

Whenever you deliver a team presentation you need to tailor what you say to the group you are addressing and make sure that you use encouraging and motivating language that will make the team members feel valued.

Motivate in the Long Term

Shouting, pleading, and insulting may be good ways to get a football team fired up to give everything they have for a short 90-minute burst of effort. However, motivating a team in the workplace demands long-term effort and requires subtler and more complex forms of encouragement. If you motivate people properly you will have a team of stakeholders rather than a group of time servers.

A motivated team will be a productive team

Encourage Feedback

You need to show how much you value your team's input by encouraging feedback. You may not want people to speak up during the team meeting, but you can set aside a time for them to talk to you, ask them to send you an

Positive Motivation Techniques

HIGH IMPACT	NEGATIVE IMPACT
• Praising individuals for effort	• Blaming specific individuals when things go wrong
• Stressing the importance to the team of the group task	• Making insulting comparisons with other groups/individuals
• Stressing the importance of individual contributions	• Failing to value the contributions of individual team members
• Setting precise goals and deadlines that are achievable	• Being vague about the team's goals and deadlines
• Showing how you expect the team to achieve its goals	• Working outside the team

Motivate for Success

Start by telling everyone involved just how important they are to the organization. If their efforts were not important you wouldn't be bothering to give a team presentation.

→ State how they will benefit from their efforts.
→ Give recognition where it's due—everyone needs to feel appreciated for what they do.
→ Be enthusiastic—show how much you care if you want others to share your enthusiasm.
→ Tell everyone what your part will be. Show them that you too are making the extra effort and working for the same goal.
→ Give them precise goals and deadlines for the new effort. Telling people to work harder or better is too vague. A stated goal and a deadline by which to achieve that goal are essential if you want to get the results you need.
→ Let them know how their renewed efforts will be judged. Without a clear means of measuring how their performance has improved they won't have a goal.

email, or set up a suggestion box. This will reinforce the message that each team member counts and that you are in this together. This is particularly important for the less outgoing members of the team.

Maintain the Advantage
The team meeting can carry on long after the team has gone back to work. If you've just praised your group or called on them to go the extra mile, let other people in the company know. An email to everyone thanking them again for their achievement or for their commitment to the next effort will underline the point. Copying your manager or other project leaders into the email will make it clear that you are promoting your team within the organization.

Coach and Counsel

No matter what you do in life you will find that you sometimes need to help people with their problems. Good coaching and counseling will help others to achieve their goals.

What Is Coaching?

Team talks are the most obvious means of coaching your team, but if you are to encourage your colleagues to achieve great things you'll need to do more than just address them occasionally. It is essential that you convey to them on frequent occasions that:

Counseling promotes personal development

- You believe in their ability.
- You value their work.
- Your success is dependent on their success.
- You will be there to help and encourage them to get what they want and need.
- You want them to succeed as much as they do.

Key Counseling Skills

The key skills in counseling are those of active listening and empathizing. It is important for the person being counselled to have confidence and trust in the counselor. An effective counselor will be able to:

→ Offer real support to those needing help.
→ Promise (and maintain) confidentiality.
→ Encourage people to take steps to self-help.
→ Encourage them to seek professional help when necessary.

Team bonding outings, team T-shirts, and reward all have their part to play in creating team spirit, but

Listen and Empathize A good coach or counselor needs to be able to listen actively, empathize and allow people to come to their own decisions.

only if these five points are made clearly and often. You should look for opportunities to reemphasize them, repeating your belief to others, commenting on challenges and successes, and giving feedback about goals and the steps taken to achieve them.

What Is Counseling?

Counseling is about helping people to come to their own decisions about what they should do next to solve their problems. Workplace counseling isn't about offering solutions or reinventing yourself as a therapist or expert, but it's a way of communicating that helps people arrive at their own decisions. It can also show them how to deal with similar problems in the future.

TIP Create visible reminders of team goals in the office. Scoreboards, graphs, or "thermometers" that show progress will help keep teams focused.

Make Meetings Matter

Meetings can provide the most crucial and creative means of communication in the workplace. They can also be a complete waste of time. You have the power to decide which way it will go.

Understand the Purpose of Meetings

Too many meetings waste time because they don't have a clear purpose. A meeting is about collaboration and interaction with others. If your meetings are all about giving information or updates then consider other means of doing that, such as newsletters or email. For useful collaboration to occur you need to establish:

- **What is the goal?** Without a purpose, or a specific goal, the meeting is pointless.
- **Is there a better way?** Is a meeting really the only way to do this? Could a phone call, a conference call, an on-line discussion, or a memo do the job better?
- **What's the agenda?** Without an agenda contributors cannot be sure of the goal and structure.

What's the Agenda?

An agenda gives structure to a meeting and encourages people to focus on it—especially if their names feature on it. Even a free-form meeting like a brainstorming session can benefit from having an agenda that explains:

→ What the subject of the meeting is
→ Who will start the proceedings
→ Who will be present at the meeting
→ Who is expected to make the first suggestions/observations
→ How long the meeting is expected to last.

 TALKING TO GROUPS

- **Are all the right people attending?** If one key person is missing, the meeting will probably generate another meeting. Check availability before calling a meeting.
- **Are they ready?** Give advance warning of the goal and the agenda and stress the nature and importance of each person's expected contribution. Make it clear what is expected of them and they will arrive focused and ready to perform.
- **Are they aware of the importance of a result?** Make sure that everyone understands what the consequences will be if the meeting doesn't produce a result.

Aim for a Resolution from Every Meeting

One of the problems with meetings is that they can get in the way of seeing the real goals, which means that people often don't take them seriously. If everyone involved realizes the consequences of a meeting's failure to produce a successful resolution the meeting's real importance becomes clear. This will also help to cut down on the number of meetings that resolve to have another meeting.

The least productive people are usually the ones who are most in favor of holding meetings.

Thomas Sowell

Make an Impact

When you go into a meeting be clear about your goal and seize the moment to make your point. People fail to contribute to meetings for a variety of reasons: shyness, nerves, lack of preparation, and a cynical conviction that the whole thing is a waste of time. These reasons become self-fulfilling prophecies. If you are too nervous to speak people will learn to stop asking your opinion; if you fail to prepare you will fail; and if you go into a meeting convinced it will be a waste of time, then it will be. A good chairperson, well structured meetings, and an open corporate culture all contribute to good meetings, but you alone are responsible for making your meetings matter—so try to break the negative cycle of apathy .

Take Center Stage

If you have something to say don't just slip it into the discussion. Announce yourself with an introductory statement, such as "I'm very glad we're here today to talk about this because I have been working on a solution to exactly this problem."

Be Confident Making a presentation with confidence is a good way to persuade people to support your goals.

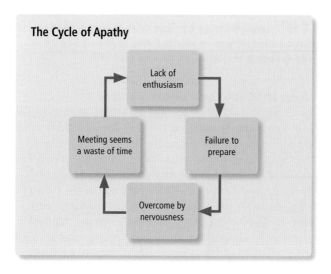

The Cycle of Apathy

Lack of enthusiasm

Failure to prepare

Overcome by nervousness

Meeting seems a waste of time

This should fix attention on you and your proposal. If you don't have a proposal

Break the Cycle Whether it's your meeting or someone else's, it's in your power to make it a good one.

to make, avoid thinking that you can take a back seat and be completely passive. Make sure you note the key points, and then, rather than allowing presentations to drift on, step in and ask if you can summarize to ensure that you have understood. Repeat the key points as you see them and ask if you've got it right. Done properly, this shows that you are paying attention, and it also prevents presentations going on longer than necessary. Keep everyone focused on the final goal, and ask whether the proposal you have summarized will achieve that. Instead of throwing the question out to the whole meeting, maintain control by asking specific individuals for input. Then ask if everyone in attendance agrees with this input.

TIP Talk about "us" and "we" rather than "you" and "I." Emphasize that you are including everyone by making eye contact with all present.

TIP Always arrive on time for a meeting that you have called. If you're late it looks as if you don't take the meeting seriously, so no one else will.

Keep It Simple and Under Control

Don't be tempted to say too much. People's attention span is limited and they are more likely to listen attentively to a short speech. Make your point as clearly as you can and don't expand on it unless specifically asked to. If it is more than a simple one-line statement, then have a short summary ready and end with a description of the impact your proposal would have, if carried. Use scenarios and real examples to illustrate your point. If you are chairing the meeting remember that you are in charge and it is your job to stop other people from getting off the topic, being irrelevant, or hijacking the meeting altogether. It is possible to bring people gently back to the subject without appearing rude. Make it clear that you are acting on behalf of others: "That's an excellent point, but for the engineers present could you show how that will affect the project?"

CASE study: Improving the Focus

Karen, the sales director for a large software producer, routinely found that her highly intelligent but easily distracted team lacked focus during meetings, leading to shapeless discussions that ran over the allotted time. She experimented with putting up large signs in the meeting room that asked questions such as "What is the purpose of the meeting?" "Have I fulfilled my role in the meeting?" "Am I sufficiently prepared?" Soon her meetings were focused, productive, and beginning and ending punctually.

• *Karen's signs were a constant reminder of the purpose of the meetings and helped everyone to focus on the matter in hand.*
• *By stressing that everyone present was part of the meeting, her tactic encouraged them to improve their performance.*

Learn to Chair

Even the most informal brainstorming sessions benefit from being well led. By honing your skills as chairperson you will show leadership, get the most from every meeting, and ensure that everyone is heard.

Successful meetings will always be lively and spontaneous but they still need structure and a guiding hand if they are to reach a successful conclusion. The two most important factors to consider when planning a meeting are who should be in attendance and what should be discussed—the purpose of the meeting.

→ Issue written invitations to ensure that everyone who needs to be at a meeting will be there, and nobody else.

→ Attach an agenda to each invitation, so that the attendees know in advance what is going to be discussed, and in what order the items will be dealt with. This will enable them to have to hand any reports or material that they will need.

Effective Foundations

DOS	DON'TS
• Do schedule meetings to take place at times and on days when you're most likely to achieve maximum attendance and interest.	• Don't schedule meetings for during or just after lunch, Monday mornings, Friday afternoons, or outside normal working hours.
• Do timetable all meetings to take place during the working day.	• Don't invite people who have no reason to attend the meeting.
• Do make the goal of the meeting clear to everyone who will attend.	• Don't allow a meeting to be open-ended—this will encourage people to ramble off the point.
• Do state how long the meeting is expected to last, and start and finish at the appointed time.	• Don't entertain late-comers by holding up the start of the meeting until they arrive.
• Do make it clear that being late to the meeting is unacceptable.	• Don't allow people to speak out of turn, for longer than they should, or while someone else is speaking.
• Do make everyone stick to their allotted time when speaking.	

Learn to Present Well

Presentations may seem daunting but they are in fact wonderful opportunities. They should be your moment in the limelight, a chance to showcase yourself, your ideas, and your excellent communication skills.

Have a Clear Purpose

The first step when planning a presentation is to ask what your purpose is. You need to establish some facts to get a clear idea of what needs to be in your presentation.

- Are you introducing a new product or service?
- Are you issuing a call to action?
- Are you rebutting or responding to someone else's presentation?
- Are you essentially entertainment rather than education?

Plan the Detail

Establish your purpose

Plan your presentation

Have a definite beginning

Develop your theme

Have a definite end

Put Together a Good Presentation

It's often said that the secret of presentations is to tell people what you're going to tell them, then tell them, then tell them what you've just told them. It's not a bad approach since it covers the idea of introduction, subject, and summary, but a really good presentation will go somewhat further. Start by thinking of everything you need to say and then halving it. The shorter and simpler a presentation the better its chances of success.

- **Start with a flourish**
  This could be a provocative statement, a joke, or a quote, but often the simplest and most effective approach is to ask the audience a question about the

subject and how they relate to it, or how it relates to them. The objective is to engage your audience and introduce your theme.

- **Begin at the beginning**
  Introduce yourself by telling your audience the most interesting thing about what you do.

- **Engage the interest of your audience**
  Say what you're going to talk about and why your audience should care about the topic. Let them know what's in it for them, how they will be affected, and what you will expect them to do about it at the end.

> **Presentations are excellent opportunities to impress**

- **Expand your theme**
  Bring your subject to life with examples, scenarios, case histories, and storytelling.

- **Finish effectively**
  End with a summary and make it clear you are drawing your presentation to a close. People will pay closer attention at this point, so bear in mind that if you want them to remember just one thing from the presentation this is the time to tell them that single thing.

think SMART

Make sure you have checked that you know exactly where and when you are presenting, that the venue has everything you need, and that all the electrical equipment is in working order.

Establish where the electrical points are; if there is enough seating; if the whiteboard pens work. Be sufficiently prepared so that you can still give the presentation if all of the props fail owing to power failure or other unexpected problems.

Use PowerPoint Effectively

While PowerPoint makes it relatively easy to give a presentation, it can make all presentations look much the same. Help yours to stand out by customizing it to your audience. Keep the slide count under 20, and never have more than a few lines of text on screen.

Make It to Measure

The easiest way to customize your presentation is to have a title screen that names the date and venue and identifies the audience. You could also include the organization's logo on each slide. This will make it clear that you are not just using an off-the-shelf presentation.

Profits by quarter

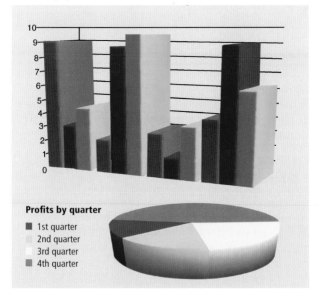

Make Use of Software Presentation software such as Microsoft PowerPoint makes it easy to create, order, and display slides on your computer. It is quick and simple to create charts such as this pie chart and bar chart, and these can be tweaked on screen until they're absolutely right for your presentation.

Making a PowerPoint presentation is more difficult than it looks and it takes a bit of practice to become fluent.

Ask a friend or colleague to make a video of you while you do a trial run.

• Make your presentation to an empty room, facing into the room (where your audience will be) while speaking.

• If you need to refer to a slide while speaking keep your body facing toward the room and gesture or half turn to the screen before turning back to face the room.

• Watch the videotape to see what your body language is saying about how much you care about your audience. Change any aspect of it that needs improvement.

Illustrate Your Presentation

It's easy to include photographs, clip art, or cartoons in a PowerPoint presentation, so why not use a digital camera to incorporate members of the audience, or photos of the product. Think about engaging your audience by using the charting function to express numbers as pie or bar charts rather than dull figures.

Use Special Effects

Animate but don't dazzle. Don't distract your audience with cartoon characters. Use instead the animation menu to bring your text to life. Select the text box on any slide and click on Animation Effects. Sliding text on to the screen is a simple way to build your argument.

• Your slide comes up with the first line of text to provide the basis for discussion.

• On your click or keystroke the next line of text appears on the slide.

By using this feature, you can control the information flow so that your audience stays with you while you are making your point rather than reading ahead.

Learn to Interact

Audience interaction, either during or after a presentation, is often the part of presenting that people dread most. It's understandable—people are unpredictable, we are afraid of being asked questions we can't answer (or, worse still, not being asked anything at all), or of someone in the audience heckling or hijacking the proceedings. Remember that you are in charge, and, if properly handled, a bit of interaction will reinforce this. Consider these different types of interaction:

- **Referring to members of the audience**
  If you have talked to members of your audience before the beginning of your presentation then mention people by name when you are under way.
- **Asking a question**
  Start the proceedings with a question—this will act to wake people up and make them concentrate on what it is that you are doing and saying.
- **Using people as props**
  Bring other people on stage with you to share their wisdom, either in person or by using short video clips.

CASE study: Waking Up the Audience

Qiang was scheduled to deliver her presentation to a sales conference in the dreaded post-lunch spot when people are sleepy and their attention wanders. She decided to use a "come on down" approach, inviting audience members to join her on stage and give their opinions. In reality she was using forewarned colleagues, but to the rest of the audience it appeared spontaneous. Fearing that any one of them might be called up on stage, everybody in the audience was suddenly awake and alert.

- *Qiang's tactic produced the liveliest question-and-answer session of the conference.*
- *All those at the conference remembered most of the detail of her presentation long afterward.*

Dealing with Audience Questions

Opening up the presentation to audience questions is an excellent strategy but one that carries some risks. Minimize their impact by taking some preemptive action.

→ Arm yourself
Try to find out whether there might be difficult questions, or whether anyone with a "pet" point of view is likely to air it.

→ Don't bluff
We all dread being asked a question we can't answer, but resist the temptation to bluff. Acknowledge that you don't have an answer but will make the effort to find out.

→ Enlist an expert
If you know you have a weak area have a specialist or a colleague on hand when difficult questions come up.

→ Avoid being sidetracked
If you think you are being sidetracked acknowledge the question ("That's an interesting point"), use it as a bridge to get back to where you were ("which shows how important this subject is"), and then return seamlessly to your subject ("which is why I am here to say that....").

Capture Their Interest You'll know that your presentation worked if you face a barrage of audience questions.

Speak in Public

A common initial reaction to an invitation to speak in public is to think of ways of avoiding it. You need to approach the experience positively and see it as an opportunity to shine rather than an ordeal.

Enjoy the Experience

Rather than thinking in terms of surviving an ordeal, think about how much you're going to enjoy the experience. Some people excel at public speaking. They are relaxed, smiling, and clearly enjoying themselves. For some people it's the most fun they ever get to have at work. You might think that they are relaxed because they know they're so good but it's just as likely that they learned to be good because they set out to enjoy themselves.

Analyze Your Fears

In order to help get over your stage fright take a moment to think about just what it is you are afraid of.

- **I'll be exposed as a fake**
  No you won't, because you're not. Nobody expects you to be a world-class orator. If you prepare a decent speech and practice it, you'll deliver it clearly and confidently.

Using boards Aim to point, turn, and then talk in order to avoid talking with your back to the audience.

- **I'll forget what I have to say**
  Everyone fears drying up, which is another very good reason to practice. Some people prefer to memorize their speech—if you can do this give a copy of your speech to a friend so that he or she can listen to you and prompt you until you are word perfect.
- **I'll make a mistake**
  We all do. Have a joke ready so that if you stumble, stutter, or have to check your notes then you can win the audience over and buy a little time to gather your thoughts and carry on.

Effective Body Language

HIGH IMPACT

- Adopting a relaxed stance
- Looking at your audience
- Moving around while you speak
- Putting your hands in your pockets occasionally

NEGATIVE IMPACT

- Standing stiffly to attention
- Looking down at your notes, or up at the ceiling
- Standing as if rooted to the spot
- Keeping your hands by your sides

Summary: Speaking to Others

Skillful speech makes all the difference when it comes to expressing yourself and convincing others. Knowing how to speak makes all the difference between empty talk and real communication, so whenever you need to motivate your team, convert sceptics, or encourage people to do better, your speaking skills will be your most useful tool.

Developing Your Speaking Skills

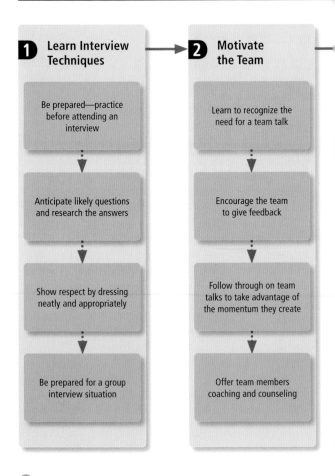

1 Learn Interview Techniques

Be prepared—practice before attending an interview

Anticipate likely questions and research the answers

Show respect by dressing neatly and appropriately

Be prepared for a group interview situation

2 Motivate the Team

Learn to recognize the need for a team talk

Encourage the team to give feedback

Follow through on team talks to take advantage of the momentum they create

Offer team members coaching and counseling

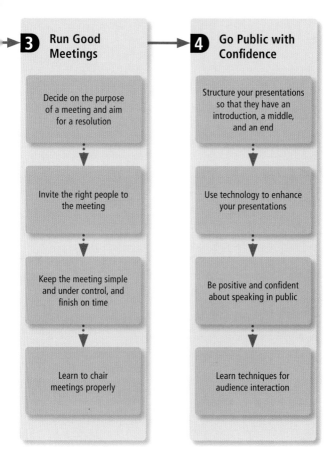

3 Run Good Meetings

Decide on the purpose of a meeting and aim for a resolution

↓

Invite the right people to the meeting

↓

Keep the meeting simple and under control, and finish on time

↓

Learn to chair meetings properly

4 Go Public with Confidence

Structure your presentations so that they have an introduction, a middle, and an end

↓

Use technology to enhance your presentations

↓

Be positive and confident about speaking in public

↓

Learn techniques for audience interaction

Managing Media 4

Communication is about much more than face-to-face discussions. We live in a world of multimedia, where we are expected to master telephones, the written word, audio and video conferencing, journalist interviews, and even television in order to get the message across. This chapter explains how to:

- Fine-tune your telephone technique
- Write good letters and emails
- Write succinct reports
- Talk to the press
- Handle television interviews

Develop a Telephone Technique

You don't have to work in a call center to benefit from good telephone technique. Good phone technique is an everyday talent that's worth tuning to perfection.

Improve Your Telephone Skills

Although much of modern business is done over the phone the belief persists that the only people who need to practice telephone technique are salespeople. We all need to hone our phone skills. A phone call is a conversation without the benefit of eye contact, facial expression, or body language. Developing a good telephone technique is the only way of compensating for this.

Take All Incoming Calls

The phone often seems like a noisy intruder, ringing just when you are in the middle of something. You may be tempted to let it ring while you finish whatever it is you are doing. However, think how impatient you feel when you call someone and the phone rings and rings. So pick up the phone as fast as you can—within three to five rings if possible. If you are

Plan Your Calls Gathering all the information you need in advance will help you to speak more confidently.

Prepare Your Outgoing Calls

Even social calls have a purpose to them, so don't be afraid to structure your calls. This will ensure that no time is wasted on either side. Prepare a precise "road map" taking you to the point you want to arrive at and what needs to be mentioned on the way. List the different stages as a series of bullet points.

→ Write down the first words you intend to say in order to state who you are and what your purpose is.
→ Include a series of questions to which you need answers.
→ Add your closing comments—are you hoping to meet up? Are you sending regards to the person's colleagues or family (you'll need to remember their names)?

sitting in front of a computer monitor then switch it off. This won't affect your work but it will remove a distraction and help you to focus on the call.

Deal with Unavailability

If the person you want to talk to is not there, or is busy, suggest a time for you to call back. This will be appreciated and your eventual discussion will start off on the right foot. Don't leave the question open, however. Suggest times for a call, asking which day and time of day would be suitable. This helps fix a time and sounds both helpful and efficient.

5 minute FIX

Calls are too important to be made randomly throughout the day.

- Draw up a schedule of the calls you need to make in the day.

- Divide them into high, medium, and low priority calls.

- Make sure the telephone numbers are handy, or are in your speed dial.

Memorable Voicemail

Voicemail has been with us for many years, yet some of the messages we leave make us sound as if we're in a state of shock. The secret of good voicemail is to speak naturally, as if you were talking to someone real.

Leaving Voicemail

Never forget that while you may be talking to a machine, the person picking up that mail will hear you speaking directly into her ear. No matter how frustrated or angry you feel, don't convey this when leaving your message.

- Be careful not to be over-familiar. Familiarity may be perfectly acceptable when leaving a message on a friend's cell phone, but it is completely inappropriate in the work context.
- Don't be surprised by voicemail. Have a message ready so that you don't sound hesitant.
- Make your message short. Few people enjoy going through their voicemail—they'll lose patience with a long message filled with irrelevant information.
- Speak clearly but fairly quickly, and to the point. Long-winded, rambling messages are likely to be deleted.
- If you're going to leave details, such as a phone number, announce it, asking if the recipient has a pen.

think SMART

People who are uncomfortable with technology often leave stilted voice messages. This will always sound unwelcoming and out of touch.

Take some time to listen to other people's messages. Note the wording and tone of those that impress you. Practice recording your message on a tape recorder and listen to your tone until you get it right. Finally, record your voicemail and check it by playing back your own message.

Good Voicemail Techniques

HIGH IMPACT

- Carefully preparing the message that you are going to leave on your voicemail
- Recording your message at a quiet time of the day—if there's a lot of noise in the background it will confuse the caller
- Standing up while speaking to enable your voice to resonate properly and make you sound more confident
- Providing an alternative contact's telephone or extension number

NEGATIVE IMPACT

- Ad libbing when recording your voicemail message
- Recording your message in a noisy office—come into work a bit earlier one morning to do it
- Sitting down while recording your message—this sometimes makes you sound too informal
- Making jokes—it will simply sound unprofessional to the caller
- Loud breathing and chewing—these will sound deafening to someone concentrating on picking up their messages

Set Up Your Voicemail

Your voicemail is your personal doorman. It can act as a shield against unwelcome callers, but you will be judged by how courteous, efficient, and friendly it is. Consider what it will say about you to your callers.

- Set your voicemail message so that it gives your name. This will reassure callers that they're through to the right person, and will encourage them to leave a message.
- Include the date in your message, even though this means updating your message daily. This will show that you haven't left the office, gone on vacation, or are out of the office. It makes it clear that you expect to return or deal with business calls on the same working day.
- When you go away leave a message saying so, remembering to update your message the day you get back, and before you get called into catch-up meetings. (Don't advertise your absence if you work from home.)
- Give callers an alternative point of contact: "If your message is urgent please call James at ...."

Write Good Letters

The written word still has immense power and in a world of rapid communication and fast-deleted messages its importance lies in its endurance.

How to Write a Letter

Letters are often studied with far greater attention to detail than emails or voicemails. This makes it all the more important to construct them carefully—a badly written letter may haunt you for a long time.

- Ask yourself why you are writing the letter. Is it a request, or a requirement, a proposition, a sales pitch, or an apology? If you are clear about what you hope the letter will achieve you are less likely to wander away from the point you are trying to make.
- Your purpose should be clear from the very first paragraph, which should introduce your point in a concise way.
- The body of the letter should develop your proposal.
- The last paragraph should explain what you hope will be the result of sending the letter.

Informality at work doesn't extend to letter writing

Get It Right

Check the formal etiquette of letter introductions, main bodies, and conclusions. This includes such rules as adding your own address and the date, as well as introductions and conclusions. Use a spellchecker if you're using a computer (cautiously, as they can be wrong), and use a good dictionary if writing by hand—a single misspelling can undermine the seriousness of an entire letter.

TIP Use the active voice. "I will send it to you" sounds much more engaged and far less pompous than the passive "It will be sent to you."

Good Beginnings and Endings

It's easy to get confused about the rules for beginning and ending business letters—remember that your concluding words will be governed by the way you start.

→ If you don't know the name of the person you're writing to, start with "Dear Sir" or "Dear Ms." and end with "Yours truly" and your initials and surname.

→ When you start with someone's name, such as "Dear George," or "Dear Mr. Blair," end with "Yours sincerely" and your first and last name.

→ The business cultures of some countries (e.g. France and Italy) expect elaborate and formulaic conclusions, even in relatively informal letters. Replacing these with something shorter and more informal will sound inappropriate.

Watch Your Apostrophes

Poor punctuation can seriously undermine your efforts and give a poor impression of you and your organization. Punctuation is there for a purpose—to clarify your message. If you are never very sure about points of punctuation, buy a small grammar book and refer to it whenever the need arises. One of the most common punctuation pitfalls is the use of the apostrophe. There are two uses for it:

1 To indicate that there are letters missing from a word: it's (for "it is"); don't (for "do not").

2 To indicate possession: John's computer (the computer that belongs to John).

Apostrophes do not indicate plurals so avoid common errors such as "CD's"; be aware of what to do with possessive plurals (people's, children's); and ensure that you always remember that "it's" never denotes possession.

Make Reports and Proposals

Reports and proposals will be scrutinized in detail and therefore require special care. Fortunately, there are well-established guidelines that will help you do this.

Write a Report

The first thing to do when asked to write a report is ask who the report is for and what its purpose is. If possible ask for a sample report on which to base yours. You should include these standard elements:

- Title, author (you), and date, followed by a detailed list of the report's contents.
- Introduction—introduces the aims of the report, and any terms of reference that may need to be spelled out. This will depend on your audience, so if you are unsure whether you need to introduce terms of reference you

Making a Proposal

In a proposal the executive summary is so important that almost everything else can be put into the appendices. The executive summary should focus very clearly on:

→ The need being addressed (or)
→ The opportunities that could be exploited
→ The way in which the proposal addresses these
→ The benefits it brings to the situation.

Just about every other element, including your track record (or your team's), the costs, the timeline, etc., should be structured so that the client can dip into them if they are interested. Clients should not be forced to wade through the details of your past achievements in order to get to the point of what you are offering them in your proposal.

probably need to ask more about who will receive the report.

Bring Figures to Life The best way to present figures in reports is visually, in charts and diagrams.

- Executive summary—no more than a page distilling the content of the report's observations and conclusions. This is the part that everyone will read in order to decide whether to delve any deeper.
- Background—explains why the report is needed.
- Body of the report—examines the events, the results of these, and their implications for the business.
- Recommendations for action—include the reasoning and most likely the risks or gains associated with each.
- Appendices.
- Acknowledgments.

Avoid the Pitfalls

Don't confuse your initial letter of proposal with the full proposal itself. Focus on the benefits of your proposal without getting lost in the details. Try not to list figures if there is any other way of showing them. Pie charts, bar charts, and diagrams can be created within packages, and these can add visual punch to proposals while making information easier to digest. Figures, diagrams, and technical detail should be included in the appendices.

Email with Impact

Email is easy, instant, and spans the world. Although it has evolved from a mixture of the written and spoken word it has its own distinct etiquette and rules.

Write Effective Emails

Emails aren't letters, and are usually scanned rather than read, so it's important to keep them brief and to the point. Emails aren't as easy to read as words on paper so it's best to stick to simple text, using plenty of spacing. Breaking messages into points and making each one a new paragraph will help keep it clear. If you are making several points then number them. Don't send an email until you have read through it. If it is a particularly important email then write it in your word processing program so that you can check it (and spell check it) at your leisure. When you are sure that you have got it right you can cut and paste the text into your email to send.

Forward with Care

When you are forwarding an email, make sure that there is nothing in the forwarded email that is not intended to be read by your recipient. Even though it may take more time, it's always better to cut and paste the salient points from the third party email into your own email.

Use Email Effectively

HIGH IMPACT

- Keeping a group up to speed with events
- Praising individuals and teams
- Acknowledging receipt of information
- Speeding up exchanges of letters/information
- Transferring electronic files

NEGATIVE IMPACT

- Hiding behind email rather than talking to people
- Sending copies to people who aren't involved in an issue
- Sending copies to senior staff you wouldn't contact otherwise
- Blocking information through constant questioning

Emailing Dos and Don'ts

Email has evolved from the written and the spoken word and, while less formal than traditional letter writing, it has its own distinct etiquette and rules.

Because we can write emails quickly, we tend to be less careful with them than with any other form of written communication. However, it is worth remembering that emails are just as permanent and irrevocable as any letter or fax that you send.

Use Correct Email Etiquette

DOS	DON'TS
• Do include the previous message when replying to make it clear what you are responding to.	• Don't use CAPITAL LETTERS—it is the email equivalent of shouting and to regular emailers it comes across as being every bit as rude.
• Do be careful not to use the "reply all" feature when the rest of the group are not concerned.	• Don't send every email marked as "urgent" or "priority". The terms will lose all meaning.
• Do run a spell check for all but the most casual emails.	
• Do make the subject line meaningful. "Hi there everyone" could come from a stranger and be about anything. "4:30 production team meeting on Monday" gives an idea of the subject and its importance.	• Don't send out jokes to groups of your friends and contacts. For many these will be unwanted and ignored, and they may even start to block your mail.
• Do acknowledge emails, especially on the first exchange, so that the recipient knows she has used the correct address.	• Don't use signature files. A signature file is a bit of text that is automatically added at the end of every message. That joke or wry quotation you once liked will get tiresome for those who receive it with each of your emails.

"

Information technology and business are becoming inextricably interwoven.

Bill Gates

"

Video and Audio Conferencing

When video and audio conferencing became technically possible the end of long-distance business travel was predicted. However, organizations that use either or both usually don't rely on them exclusively.

Pay Attention to Names

You need to pay particular attention to introductions and interactions. In a face-to-face meeting the participants greet each other as they enter the meeting room. In a video conference this is possible for each location, but particular care has to be taken about making introductions between the different remote sites. If you forget the name of someone in a face-to-face meeting you can still address comments to her by facing her and speaking to her directly. In a video or audio conference this is not possible.

- In video conferences place a large name card in front of each participant.
- In audio conferences ask people to preface their comments with their names.
- Include a facilitator who knows everyone and can introduce each person by name in the style of a TV talk show host.

Don't Be Dazzled by Technology
Video conferencing is a test of interpersonal, not technical skills.

TECHNIQUES *to* practice

Video conferencing is a very useful communication tool, allowing people in different locations to attend meetings together. However, how well you use the technology will have an impact on the quality of your meeting. Help yourself to make things go as smoothly as they possibly can by familiarizing yourself with a few basic techniques for adapting to the technology.

- Make sure you turn up 10 to 20 minutes before the conference is due to start to allow time for setting up.
- Practice looking into the camera when it's your turn to make key points.
- Place the speaker phone in the center of the participants' seating area.
- Ask everyone to speak clearly, and not too quickly, but not to shout or raise their voices.

Keep Control

The role of the chair and of the agenda are more important than ever because it is essential that no one tries to talk over anyone else. In an audio-conferencing situation this is ruder than it would be if accompanied by the body language and gestures of normal speech. From a technical standpoint it will probably cause sound delays. Stress the importance of sticking to proper meeting etiquette. Keeping to an agreed agenda helps maintain focus, and the chair will need to be firm about making sure that each person has her say and then lets others speak. Any rules about speaking and turn-taking should be established right from the start. An introductory period, during which people introduce themselves and the agenda is read, will also serve to ease people into the format.

TIP Make sure that everyone is introduced at the start. Someone who isn't introduced and then speaks up will surprise the others.

Deal with the Press Effectively

Talking to the press is a wonderful opportunity to publicize your organization, or spread the word about a project while simultaneously promoting yourself.

Prepare Well

The biggest risk you run when talking to the press is that you will be wasting your time because you haven't spent enough time analyzing what you want to achieve. Be very clear about what you have to say and why it might be of interest. Think about how you would tell your story, and practice it on a colleague. Don't presume that the journalist knows as much as you do about your subject, even if you are talking to a trade journal that specializes in it. Be prepared to explain yourself in the simplest, clearest terms possible. To make sure you are both talking the same language do a little preparation by looking at the publication and its target audience. Ideally, you should

Use simple language to communicate clearly

think SMART

!

Before you start, ask the journalist what kind of story she is working on. Most people are happy to talk about their work and knowing why you are being interviewed will help you to shape your responses.

Even if you've just been asked for an overview or an analysis of a situation, ask the journalist if she has spoken to anyone else about the subject. If she has already spoken to a rival then she is probably looking for your response to your rival's point of view. If you are aware of that you will make a better job of your interview.

Learn to Handle Telephone Interviews

Although a lot of interviews take place over the telephone this can make people nervous and they don't do as well as they would in a face-to-face situation.

→ Never feel pressured into making comments when unprepared.
→ Feel free to tell a journalist that, given a little time to put order into your ideas, you would give a much better comment.
→ Fix a later time to talk.
→ It is common to think of a great comment after the interview. Ask for the journalist's email address and make a point of mailing any further thoughts.

speak the language of the readers, whether they happen to be academics or business people. Try to use simple, plain language, even when explaining technical terms—otherwise you may have to stop halfway through an interview to think of a simpler explanation.

Take an Active Role

Be active in your approach rather than allowing yourself to be led down a line of questioning. A journalist may have missed the point and will be very happy if you stress what you think is the most interesting aspect of an issue. Don't bluff if you don't know the answer to something. Instead, make it clear that you will find out the information and pass it on. If you do promise to do something, make sure that you deliver on your promise and contact the journalist after the interview to pass on the facts. Instead of being passive and waiting for questions to answer, try suggesting what you think is the most important aspect of what you have to say. By taking the intitiative you will make the interview better for both of you.

TV and Radio Interviews

TV and radio appearances were once reserved for the rich and famous but the explosion in digital channels means that there's a good chance you will find yourself in front of the cameras or a radio microphone.

Be Confident

The ground rules for TV and radio interviews are exactly the same as for the regular press, but with a few issues of presentation on top. Although most people worry more about how they will look/sound, it is important not to forget that the foundation of any good performance is good content. If you have rehearsed your comments and know what you are talking about you will automatically appear more relaxed and confident.

- In order to make absolutely sure that what you are going to say will sound good, insist on talking to the producer or producer's assistant about what it is you are going to do. They will be able to tell you exactly how long you will be on air, what will be asked (you can sometimes suggest the precise wording yourself), and who else will be interviewed.

- If you're in a studio try not to make elaborate gestures (you will appear nervous). Fold your hands on the desk, plant the soles of your feet solidly on the floor, and take a breath before you start.

- Ask in advance how many minutes you will be speaking for and tailor what you're going to say to the time limit. If you're not used to talking on the air, three minutes might seem like an eternity.

5 minute FIX

If the prospect of appearing on television is making you nervous, just before you go on:

- Sing a few notes to warm up your voice.

- Sip a glass of water to prevent your mouth drying up.

- Take a few deep breaths so that you will feel relaxed.

If an interviewer asks you an unexpected question during an interview, prevent yourself getting tongue-tied by using the ABC technique.
In this technique A stands for Acknowledge, B for Bridge and C for Communicate. Practice the technique by asking a friend to ask you some difficult questions about a particular subject.

- Acknowledge the question by saying: "That's a very good point you've made…"

- Bridge to what you want to say: "…and it's precisely because I'm concerned about this issue …"

- Communicate your original point: "…that I'm here to tell you about my proposal."

Dress to Impress

If you're going to appear on television make sure you choose your clothes with care, always wearing neutral colors (not white) and avoiding complicated patterns, which can cause a strobing effect. Take some alternatives with you—few studios will have anything for you to wear. Pick up a few tips from TV news presenters about what looks best on screen. Television studio lights are very hot, so make sure your clothes won't show sweat. Most interviews are conducted sitting down, so sit in front of a mirror and make sure that your choice of clothes looks good and is comfortable when you sit down.

Jackets or tops that button up, as opposed to something like a T-shirt, will make it much easier to hide the wiring of microphones. Above all don't choose this time to try a new outfit—something tried and trusted is always a better bet, and will help to calm any nerves.

> **The media . . . have the power to make the innocent guilty and the guilty innocent.**
>
> Malcolm X

Summary: Handling the Media

It's easy to be distracted by the media, but the key is to remember that what is important is that the media are a direct channel to your customers. Don't let yourself be intimidated. Ignore the bright lights and recording technology, shape your message for your customers, say what you have to say—and you will shine.

Developing Your Media Skills

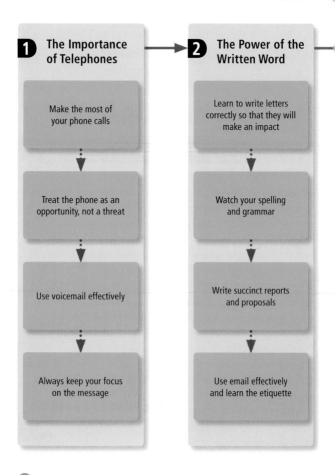

1 **The Importance of Telephones**

Make the most of your phone calls

Treat the phone as an opportunity, not a threat

Use voicemail effectively

Always keep your focus on the message

2 **The Power of the Written Word**

Learn to write letters correctly so that they will make an impact

Watch your spelling and grammar

Write succinct reports and proposals

Use email effectively and learn the etiquette

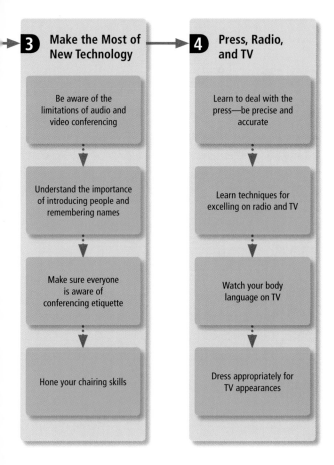

3 **Make the Most of New Technology**

Be aware of the limitations of audio and video conferencing

Understand the importance of introducing people and remembering names

Make sure everyone is aware of conferencing etiquette

Hone your chairing skills

4 **Press, Radio, and TV**

Learn to deal with the press—be precise and accurate

Learn techniques for excelling on radio and TV

Watch your body language on TV

Dress appropriately for TV appearances

Deal with 5 Conflict

Communication is all about bringing people together, but this doesn't guarantee that they will agree. A degree of conflict is inevitable in the workplace and good communication is what makes the difference between a healthy exchange of ideas and a full-on confrontation. In this chapter you will learn how to:

• Encourage and manage healthy conflict
• Identify communications breakdowns before they happen
• Resolve conflict with different techniques
• Resolve individual frictions
• Manage difficult people
• Get your team talking again

Rise to the Challenge

Because communication is a two-way process you won't always hear what you want to. That's not necessarily a bad thing, as long as you can manage the fine line between healthy and unhealthy conflict.

Be Positive

Conflict in itself is neither a good thing nor a bad thing. It's how we react to it that decides whether or not it is a healthy influence in the workplace. A certain amount of conflict is inevitable. Living with some conflict can be a lot more positive than working in an environment where nobody cares enough to have any conflict at all. Managed well, conflict can be productive, can draw people together, and can contribute to an understanding of viewpoints and depth of feeling. Managed badly, however, and that conflict can lead to hostility, resentment, estrangement, and a communications breakdown. According to professional survey, managing conflict at work costs the average employer nearly 450 days of management time every year—this can be equated to the employment of two full-time managers.

Healthy Conflict Conflict between those who trust and respect each other can be a positive force at work.

Keep the Balance

Encouraging healthy conflict while avoiding confrontation is a balancing act but there are certain things you can do to ensure that conflict is kept at healthy levels.

→ Encourage coworkers to voice their differences of opinion. Ask the opinion of others before you venture your own, and be sure that you show sufficient respect to those whose ideas you don't agree with.

→ Thank people for being prepared to stand up and disagree with a group, or question the consensus. Make it clear that you expect different opinions to be backed up with convincing arguments and relevant facts. You're not there to provide a platform for those who are simply opinionated. That doesn't mean you don't value their opinions, it just means that you want them to be substantiated.

→ Set as a ground rule that opinions or beliefs must relate clearly to the communal goal being discussed.

→ Set time limits for each speaker if some people tend to dominate at the expense of others.

Keep Control

One way of dealing with conflict is to organize a debate between the parties involved in the conflict. A structured debate doesn't have to be stuffy but you will need to ensure that it doesn't turn into a shouting match. Try controlling it with football referee-style cards. Everyone is given a card and, if an individual is being too negative, or irrelevant, then any of the others in the group can show him a warning card. After a certain number of warnings the offending individual must stop talking. This is a good way of persuading people to take a calm and rational approach in a conflict situation.

Recognize Breakdown

Breakdowns in communication, particularly in the workplace, can be subtle and progressive so it pays to learn to recognize them before they turn into shouting matches with little hope of a good outcome.

Look Out for the Signs

A certain amount of friction is inevitable wherever more than one person is working on the same project, but there are certain signs to look out for that will suggest a gap in understanding, and in particular a gap that is now interfering with people's ability to work. Likely scenarios include:

- Personality clashes
- Misunderstandings about goals
- Generation gaps
- Presumptions about the understanding of others
- Confusion and lack of direction
- Personal/hidden agendas.

Managed conflict can be a good thing

See the Humor

Humor is one of the best methods of dealing with conflict, not just as a cure, but also as a diagnostic tool. Listen carefully to the tone of office jokes as they often reveal unspoken feelings. If nobody ever voices disagreement it can mean that there is a "yes" culture in which people believe that their opinions don't matter. Critical jokes, sarcasm about people or the goals of the organization, even eye-rolling and exaggerated exasperation about people or projects are very revealing. They may be part of a team-bonding ritual, but those little jokes shouldn't be ignored—they are often based on an assumption or criticism that may one day grow out of proportion.

> **If you're the boss and people fight openly when they think that you are wrong—that's healthy.**
>
> Robert Townsend

Keep an Eye on Meetings

The way people meet is also a symptom of the communications health of the group. A tendency to open, ad hoc meetings is usually a good thing. Closed-door meetings of small groups may hint at a growing tribalism within the organization, where a section of the workforce feels its goals are not shared by others. Secret meetings, or meetings that are regularly scheduled off-site or out of hours, may not necessarily mean there is a communications breakdown, but they soon will if others feel excluded from the group and kept out of the loop.

Look at the Details

Watch out for people becoming disproportionately excited about such things as parking spaces, room layout, and desk allocation. While this might simply be a matter of ego, it can also highlight insecurities about function and importance which may mean that people need greater guidance and coaching. Watch the tone of emails and who is or isn't copied in on the lists to get a feel for any developing "us and them" culture.

CASE study: Dealing with Potential Conflict

Francesca managed both the product design team and the sales team. The work of the teams was totally separate, but they had gone further and created artificial barriers. Each team socialized in different venues, and each emailed jokes only within their team. While reading the teams' emails Francesca realized that both teams had created the illusion that only their own team's work was important to the organization. She implemented feedback meetings on product sales where key members of both teams were present.

• *Sales helped the design team understand what customers wanted, and design helped sales understand the unique features of their products.*
• *Tensions eased, and the rivalry continued but became friendlier.*
• *The organization benefited from the sharing of ideas.*

Resolve Conflict

Achieving conflict resolution can be as simple as bringing about a change of attitude. Much conflict has its roots in a lack of communication so, as a communicator, you're ideally placed to resolve it.

Analyze the Perception

Conflict usually occurs because people think they have opposing needs or desires. The perception is enough to create friction and where that interferes with work performance it becomes a question of communication. Resolving such conflict requires both an investigation into what the perceptions are, then having a discussion to establish if the perceptions have a real basis. Frequently it is the perception alone that is the problem.

Use Feedback to Avoid Conflict

Feedback is essential to good communication and provides a first line of defence against future communication breakdowns. If others have no formal way of voicing their feelings, or letting you know how they view what you have said, then you are dictating, not communicating. Set up suggestion boxes, create an on-line bulletin board to encourage comment and debate, and interview people as part of a review process. This will help harvest information while giving people a "safety-valve" for strong feelings.

Effective Ways to Deal with Problems

HIGH IMPACT	NEGATIVE IMPACT
• Acknowledging that a problem exists	• Ignoring the problem
• Identifying the problem	• Assuming that you know what the problem is
• Discussing the problem with those involved	• Broadcasting the problem throughout the organization
• Being impartial in your assessment of the problem	• Taking sides or otherwise showing favoritism

Conflict Management

There are four key approaches to dealing with conflict and breakdown. Used appropriately, these allow a framework for the management and resolution of most conflicts.

Communication Unfortunately, basic misunderstandings are the cause of many conflicts in both personal and professional situations. Lack of communication can lead to people misreading a situation. Taking time to talk together one-on-one can help to resolve these conflicts.

Negotiation Negotiation is the key tool to use when two or more parties face disagreement and need to reach an agreement that is satisfactory to all sides. It requires both parties to state their case, listen to the other side, then move towards a compromise that will bring about a win-win situation.

Mediation Where two parties are unable to reach a consensus themselves they may ask a third party to facilitate discussions. As a mediator you should remain neutral, listen to both sides, and help them move towards common ground. Sometimes it may be necessary to speak to each party separately.

Arbitration When mediation fails to produce agreement you might have to turn to an independent third party who has the authority to rule on the issue of disagreement, like a referee in sports. However, lack of consultation may leave one or more parties with long-standing grievances.

Pass on Bad News

Nobody wants to be the bearer of bad news but often there is just no choice. It is one of the greatest tests of your ability to communicate well under pressure.

Do It Now

When there's bad news to pass on we all look for someone else to do the job. There are many reasons for this reaction:

Bad news usually has no soft edges to cushion it

- We fear being blamed.
- We are concerned about the feelings of the other person.
- We don't want to be associated with the bad news.

The longer you put off telling someone bad news, the greater the chance that he will find out from another source—the consequences of that could be far worse for you. If you have news that you are worried about delivering then it almost certainly merits being delivered

TECHNIQUES *to* practice

Before you break bad some bad news to someone think about how you should go about doing it.

Be particularly careful about your tone of voice—you may want to sound reserved but a very formal approach may sound uncaring.

- Decide exactly what information you need to share, and have any necessary facts or figures to hand.

- Think about any arguments or objections that the recipient may make and how you can counter them.

- Rehearse the exact words you will use when breaking the news and repeat them aloud to decide whether you will sound convincing.

- Choose a time and a place to break the news that will provide privacy and some peace and quiet.

CASE study: Breaking the News Gradually

Knowing that layoffs were likely, Jenny, the managing director, decided to break the news in a structured way. She visited the departments likely to be affected, speaking to people individually and spelling out the bigger picture, so that people wouldn't feel that layoffs were a personal slight. She also invited suggestions for alternatives, and proposed a voluntary layoff package so that the numbers forced to leave would be reduced. She listened to everybody's angry reactions.

- *When the layoffs were announced, people were prepared for them, and many of them had the opportunity to find employment elsewhere.*
- *Jenny's tactics meant that people felt that they had been consulted about the situation.*

personally. If the news that is being broken is likely to promote an emotional response then it is important to give the recipient an outlet. If you deliver it in person you will be able to help calm the storm.

Do It Properly

Start by warning the other person that you are there to break bad news. Communicate clearly, get straight to the point, and give precise facts. Be ready to discuss, even if you think there is nothing more to be said—you must at least hear the other person's point of view. Stay calm and don't take the recipient's anger personally. Encourage him to focus on the situation or the information rather than on you. Life goes on and it's important that the bad news be seen in perspective, so that the focus can return to how to move forward from that point. The recipient of the bad news will focus on the negative. If you do likewise who is going to help you both get moving again?

TIP Try to avoid giving people bad news just before a weekend or holiday as they will dwell on it.

Deal with Friction

There will always be difficult people in life but good communication can go a long way towards smoothing the way and even removing misunderstandings that would otherwise interfere with relationships.

Face Up to It

We've all worked with someone who drove us up the wall, or whose manner irritated us. Unless you work on your own, friction with colleagues is inevitable. In order to prevent the problem from escalating, it is vital to acknowledge that the problem exists. Many of us simply don't deal with friction, we internalize our frustration and get angry, then we swallow our anger until we can let off steam with friends and partners. In an office situation it's very common to deal with a frustrating individual by seeking the solace of group opinion. How many coffee breaks are dominated by discussions about difficult people?

Talk About It Unchecked friction can damage relationships. Sit down and talk before things get out of hand.

think SMART

Instead of always seeing your problems as being someone else's fault, take responsibility for them yourself. If you allow yourself to be angered by someone else, then you are the problem.

Saying that something is all about someone else is a way of saying they have power over you. By taking the responsibility on to your own shoulders you can start to think about how you can stop being irritated, or what has caused the sore point that the other person is aggravating. Think about what you can do to stop being angered by what someone does, or about how you can rise above the other person's behavior.

Talk About It

Sometimes living with friction is the only option. More often, though, it is just the easiest. Instead of ignoring a personality issue, try to sit down and talk to the person concerned about it. It's often assumed that if the problematic person is the boss then there's no choice but to put up with it. That's not always the case, however. If individuals are not "team players" or are insecure or under pressure, then look at ways of including them in (or making them aware of) the team spirit. Remember, though, that some people have an abrasive attitude that can be difficult to live with but doesn't actually convey what they are really thinking.

5 minute FIX

If someone is annoying you and you want to avoid a confrontation:

- Ask yourself whether he's reacting to a perceived provocation on your part.

- Suggest that you may be rubbing him or her the wrong way.

- Encourage him to point out what his problem with you is.

- Listen actively and repeat his points back to him.

Deal with Team Conflict

In an ideal world your hard work on team talks, motivation, and coaching would be enough to ensure smooth teamwork. However, whenever individuals come together as a team, there will be communication issues.

Be Aware of the Complexities

Team conflict may be an extension of personal conflict, or it could be down to that complex interaction between people known as group dynamics.
Any unhealthy conflict will reduce the effectiveness of your team and will require you to step in. Communicating your way through team conflict requires all the skills needed to manage problems with individuals, but with the added complexity of group dynamics (the way that people behave in combination with others) and the obvious issue that there are more people to deal with at the same time.

Talking is the first step in conflict resolution

Get to the Root of the Problem

Start off by meeting with everyone in the team individually. This will enable you to find out what the problem really is (in a team this is often quite complex) and will give you a chance to assure everyone that you are not there to take sides or apportion blame. Ask people:

- What is going wrong
- What they think is the answer to the problem
- What they want to see management do about it.

Ask them if there is anything else they think you need to know in order to understand the problem. Thank them for helping you to understand the problem and tell them that they will have their chance to present those opinions to the group in a follow-up meeting. This prepares everyone for their time before the others and helps them to feel valued (which may be what the conflict is all about).

Resolve Conflict as a Group

Bring together the people who are in conflict and spell out the importance of solving the problem, re-emphasizing the goals and objectives of the team.

→ Have each person in turn explain what he thinks the problem is. Make sure everyone gets the time to talk without being interrupted by anyone else.

→ Don't be drawn into who is right or wrong; this is mediation, not judgment. The point is to make both parties understand the viewpoint of the other, not to score points.

→ Ask them in turn to describe what would resolve the problem. This might be management action, or it might be requests for less of one thing and more of another.

→ Engage everyone in a discussion of the changes to be adopted, and get them to commit to such changes.

→ End on a positive note, expressing your faith in the ability of the team to work out the problem itself.

Discuss the Problem Conflict occurs wherever there is a team. Learn to deal with it well and it can be a positive and constructive force.

Learn to Resolve Conflict

Your communication skills are often all that is required to iron out conflicts and get everyone "on board." Sometimes, however, your skills could do with a little help. Try coaching, negotiation, mediation, or arbitration. Make sure that you use the right technique for the situation.

Use Coaching, Team Talks, and Feedback

Coaching and team talks help bring people together, motivate them, and let them know what is expected of them. If you have frequent team talks and make coaching available to people, they are far more likely to take a constructive and non-confrontational approach to any conflict that does arise. Provide feedback channels so that grievances have no opportunity to germinate.

Use Your Negotiation Skills

Negotiation takes place when those involved discuss an issue directly with each other in the search for an outcome that will benefit everyone. It requires all parties to a

Use Training

Training has a useful role in conflict resolution. The training does not have to be specifically focused on conflict resolution in order to help. Thorough job training will go a long way to helping communications simply by making sure that everyone knows what is expected of them. Some managers don't pay enough attention to training, failing to acknowledge that:

→ Training is a great way of bringing people together and getting them "on board."
→ Lack of attention to training often paves the way for poor communication at a later date.

CASE study: Getting to the Root Cause

Patrick and Susan, both senior executives in a marketing company, had reached the point of hostile disagreement where they avoided each other in corridors and only ever spoke via other people. David, the human resources manager, had been trained in mediation and decided to step in. Patrick and Susan agreed to attend a series of meetings. Both were to have their say without interruption and the other person would repeat back what he or she had heard. After several meetings precise problems emerged: Susan felt discriminated against on the grounds of her sex, while Patrick felt that Susan was undermining his authority.

• *By bringing the problems into the open, Patrick and Susan were able to address them. By sharing their mutual concerns they also managed to build bridges.*
• *Communication improved and the whole organization felt the pervading tension ease.*

dispute to step back from the situation and consider the issue calmly and objectively. In a situation where the conflict has become so entrenched that this isn't possible mediation may be required.

Mediate to Achieve a Solution

Mediation revolves around a neutral third party who helps those involved come to their own resolution to a dispute. That's usually done by creating an atmosphere where both sides can voice their needs and wants and by encouraging them to supply those for each other.

Recognize the Need for Arbitration

Sometimes people are simply unable to settle a conflict between themselves. When this happens a third party can be called in to review the case, weigh up the arguments on both sides, and then issue a ruling which is imposed on all concerned. It is always preferable if people can resolve conflict themselves, so arbitration should be explored only when all other methods of resolution have failed.

Repair Public Relations

However big or small your organization, and whatever line of business you are in, your name, your brand, and your reputation are being discussed right now.

Recognize the Importance of PR

Public relations isn't just a matter for giant corporations, it's an issue for any company or enterprise that presents a face to the outside world. The public doesn't have to be international, or even national, and could consist of a very small group of your customers, and your own industry.

Adapt to the Situation

Taking care of public image is something that companies often agree on in principle, but hesitate to do in practice. The difficulty is that public image was once relatively easy to control. If you didn't want to talk about something, the media had nothing to go on. That's changed, however. Communications are now lightning fast and people can make contact with the entire world. Furthermore, email and on-line discussion sites mean that every customer and consumer is now a potential publisher with the ability to spread the word.

> **Public relations is all about dialogue**

Techniques to Limit the Damage

HIGH IMPACT	NEGATIVE IMPACT
• Arranging a press conference	• Refusing to comment
• Taking time to consider your response	• Responding in the heat of the moment
• Acknowledging that there is an issue to respond to	• Ignoring a situation that needs a response
• Appointing a spokesperson	• Refusing to involve your team
• Preparing a considered response	• Talking to the press ad lib

Assess Your Needs

There are companies that don't have to worry about their image among customers, but not many. The important thing therefore is to ensure that an individual or a group of people has responsibility for communicating with the outside world. Depending on the scale of your needs that could be:

→ A professional PR agency
→ A part-time specialist
→ A full-time in-house position
→ An ad hoc role undertaken by a staff member.

Public relations covers a huge area, from addressing the press to lobbying key individuals, but no review of the communications methods of any organization can afford to ignore the way in which it communicates with its own customers.

Think of the Global Audience

The greatest revolution ushered in by the worldwide web is not about technology; it's about the relationship between organizations and consumers, and good communications has to take that into account. Once the public was largely seen as passive and receptive—organizations sent out messages via advertising which were then received by the public. The only feedback was whether or not they bought the products or services. Now, however, people can email friends about their opinions, or form chat groups and bulletin boards to discuss issues. News of bad products and unethical companies spreads like wildfire.

TIP Be proactive: don't wait for the media or rumor machine to come and find you out.

Summary: Dealing with Conflict

Conflict doesn't have to be a bad thing. Properly handled, it can even be a force for good, ensuring a reappraisal of working practices and encouraging creativity. The trick is to avoid head-on confrontation and instead look for a way to express the issues in such a way that people will move forward and concentrate on achieving management goals.

Making the Best of a Situation

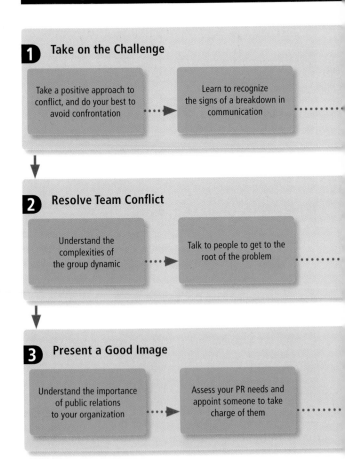

1 Take on the Challenge

Take a positive approach to conflict, and do your best to avoid confrontation ·····▶ Learn to recognize the signs of a breakdown in communication ··········

2 Resolve Team Conflict

Understand the complexities of the group dynamic ·····▶ Talk to people to get to the root of the problem ··········

3 Present a Good Image

Understand the importance of public relations to your organization ·····▶ Assess your PR needs and appoint someone to take charge of them ··········

Learn techniques for dealing with conflict and friction ┈┈┈▶ Learn the best way to break bad news to someone

Use coaching, counseling, negotiation, and mediation ┈┈┈▶ If all else fails, bring in arbitrators

Be aware of the global audience ┈┈┈▶ Pre-empt scandal, rumor, and bad publicity

Index

Picture Credits

The publisher would like to thank the following for their kind permission to reproduce their photographs: Abbreviations key: (l) = left, (c) = center, (r) = right, (t) = top, (b) = below, (cl) = center left, (cr) = center right.

1: Neil Farrin/Stone/Getty (l), Fisher/Thatcher/Stone/Getty (c), VEER Mark Adams/Photonica/Getty (r); **2:** Altrendo Images/Getty; **3:** Michael Hemsley (t), Kaz Chiba/Stone/Getty (c), Justin Pumfrey/Iconica/Getty (b); **5:** Michael Hemsley; **7:** Double Exposure/Taxi /Getty; **8:** Michael Hemsley (l), Stewart Charles Cohen/Jupiter Images (cl), Michael Hemsley (cr), Terry Vine/Stone /Getty (r); **13:** Kaz Chiba/Stone/Getty; **20:** Justin Pumfrey/Iconica/Getty; **23:** Michael Hemsley; **24:** Michael Hemsley; **28:** VEER Mark Adams/Photonica/Getty; **32:** VEER Mark Adams/Photonica/Getty; **33:** Michael Hemsley; **41:** Neil Farrin/Stone/Getty; **43:** Stewart Charles Cohen/Jupiter Images; **44:** Michael Hemsley; **51:** Double Exposure/Taxi/Getty; **53:** Romilly Lockyer /Getty; **57:** Michael Hemsley; **61:** Double Exposure/Taxi/Getty; **64:** Michael Hemsley; **73** Michael Hemsley; **74:** Fisher/Thatcher/Stone/Getty; **77:** Thomas Barwick/Getty; **79:** Hamish Blair/Reportage/Getty; **80:** Michael Hemsley; **87:** Getty; **90:** Fisher/Thatcher/Stone/Getty; **97:** Hamish Blair/Reportage/Getty; **99:** Daniel Berehulak/Reportage/Getty; **100:** Michael Hemsley; **105:** Paul Barton/Corbis (tl), Jen Petreshock/The Image Bank/Getty (tr), NO RESULT 42-15763326/Corbis (bl), Mike Hewitt/Allsport Concepts/Getty (br); **108:** Michael Hemsley; **111:** Terry Vine/Stone/Getty; **117:** VEER Mark Adams/Photonica/Getty.

All other images © Dorling Kindersley.

For further information see www.dkimages.com

Author's Biography

Steve Shipside is a writer and a consultant specializing in business and communications in the UK. Steve has written extensively on these subjects for newspapers including *The Guardian*, *The Times*, and *Telegraph*, and has authored several books, including *E-Marketing* (Capstone Express, 2001), *Podcasting* (Infinite Ideas, 2005), and DK's *Worklife: Perfect Your Presentations* (2006). Steve was a presenter on *Blue Chip*, a business and technology program on Sky TV.